YOUR PERSONAL
HOROSCOPE
2008

ARIES

YOUR PERSONAL
HOROSCOPE
2008

ARIES
21st March–20th April

igloo

igloo

This edition published by Igloo Books Ltd,
Cottage Farm, Mears Ashby Road, Sywell, Northants NN6 0BJ
www.igloo-books.com
E-mail: Info@igloo-books.com

Produced for Igloo Books by W. Foulsham & Co. Ltd,
The Publishing House, Bennetts Close, Cippenham,
Slough, Berkshire SL1 5AP, England

ISBN: 978-1-845-61619-9

Copyright © 2007 W. Foulsham & Co. Ltd

This is an abridged version of material
originally published in *Old Moore's Horoscope
and Astral Diary*.

Printed in China

CONTENTS

CONTENTS

INTRODUCTION

Your Personal Horoscopes have been specifically created to allow you to get the most from astrological patterns and the way they have a bearing on not only your zodiac sign, but nuances within it. Using the diary section of the book you can read about the influences and possibilities of each and every day of the year. It will be possible for you to see when you are likely to be cheerful and happy or those times when your nature is in retreat and you will be more circumspect. The diary will help to give you a feel for the specific 'cycles' of astrology and the way they can subtly change your day-to-day life. For example, when you see the sign ☿, this means that the planet Mercury is retrograde at that time. Retrograde means it appears to be running backwards through the zodiac. Such a happening has a significant effect on communication skills, but this is only one small aspect of how the Personal Horoscope can help you.

With Your Personal Horoscope the story doesn't end with the diary pages. It includes simple ways for you to work out the zodiac sign the Moon occupied at the time of your birth, and what this means for your personality. In addition, if you know the time of day you were born, it is possible to discover your Ascendant, yet another important guide to your personal make-up and potential.

Many readers are interested in relationships and in knowing how well they get on with people of other astrological signs. You might also be interested in the way you appear to very different sorts of individuals. If you are such a person, the section on Venus will be of particular interest. Despite the rapidly changing position of this planet, you can work out your Venus sign, and learn what bearing it will have on your life.

Using Your Personal Horoscope you can travel on one of the most fascinating and rewarding journeys that anyone can take – the journey to a better realisation of self.

THE ESSENCE OF ARIES

Exploring the Personality of Aries the Ram

(21ST MARCH – 20TH APRIL)

What's in a sign?

Aries is not the first sign of the zodiac by accident. It's the place in the year when the spring begins, and so it represents some of the most dynamic forces in nature, and within the zodiac as a whole. As a result the very essence of your nature is geared towards promoting yourself in life and pushing your ideas forward very positively. You don't brook a great deal of interference in your life, but you are quite willing to help others as much as you can, provided that to do so doesn't curb your natural desire to get on in life.

Aries people are not universally liked, though your true friends remain loyal to you under almost any circumstances. But why should it be that such a dynamic and go-getting person does meet with some opposition? The answer is simple: not everyone is quite so sure of themselves as you are and many tend to get nervous when faced with the sheer power of the Aries personality. If there is one factor within your own control that could counter these problems it is the adoption of some humility – that commodity which is so important for you to dredge from the depths of your nature. If you only show the world that you are human, and that you are well aware of the fact, most people would follow you willingly to the very gates of hell. The most successful Aries subjects know this fact and cultivate it to the full.

Your executive skills are never in doubt and you can get almost anything practical done whilst others are still jumping from foot to foot. That's why you are such a good organiser and are so likely to be out there at the front of any venture. Adventurous and quite willing to show your bravery in public, you can even surprise yourself sometimes with the limits you are likely to go to in order to reach solutions that seem right to you.

Kind to those you take to, you can be universally loved when working at your best. Despite this there will be times in your life when you simply can't understand why some people just don't like you. Maybe there's an element of jealousy involved.

Aries resources

The part of the zodiac occupied by the sign of Aries has, for many centuries, been recognised as the home of self-awareness. This means that there isn't a person anywhere else in the zodiac that has a better knowledge of self than you do. But this isn't necessarily an intellectual process with Aries, more a response to the very blood that is coursing through your veins. Aries' success doesn't so much come from spending hours working out the pros and cons of any given course of action, more from the thrill of actually getting stuck in. If you find yourself forced into a life that means constantly having to think everything through to the tiniest detail, there is likely to be some frustration in evidence.

Aries is ruled by Mars, arguably the most go-getting of all the planets in the solar system. Mars is martial and demands practical ways of expressing latent power. It also requires absolute obedience from subordinates. When this is forthcoming, Aries individuals are the most magnanimous people to be found anywhere. Loyalty is not a problem and there have been many instances in history when Aries people were quite willing to die for their friends if necessary.

When other people are willing to give up and go with the flow, you will still be out there pitching for the result that seems most advantageous to you. It isn't something you can particularly control and those who don't know you well could find you sometimes curt and over-demanding as a result. But because you are tenacious you can pick the bones out of any situation and will usually arrive at your desired destination, if you don't collapse with fatigue on the way.

Routines, or having to take life at the pace of less motivated types, won't suit you at all. Imprisonment of any sort, even in a failed relationship, is sheer torture and you will move heaven and earth to get out into the big, wide world, where you can exploit your natural potential to the full. Few people know you really well because you don't always explain yourself adequately. The ones who do adore you.

Beneath the surface

Whereas some zodiac signs are likely to spend a great deal of their lives looking carefully at the innermost recesses of their own minds, Aries individuals tend to prefer the cut and thrust of the practical world. Aries people are not natural philosophers, but that doesn't mean that you aren't just as complicated beneath the surface as any of your astrological brothers and sisters. So what is it that makes the Aries firebrand think and act in the way that it does? To a great extent it is a lack of basic self-confidence.

This statement might seem rather odd, bearing in mind that a fair percentage of the people running our world were born under the sign of the Ram, but it is true nevertheless. Why? Because people who know themselves and their capabilities really well don't feel the constant need to prove themselves in the way that is the driving force of your zodiac sign. Not that your naturally progressive tendencies are a fault. On the contrary, if used correctly they can help you to create a much better, fairer and happier world, at least in your own vicinity.

The fact that you occasionally take your ball and go home if you can't get your own way is really down to the same insecurity that is noticeable through many facets of your nature. If Aries can't rule, it often doesn't want to play at all. A deep resentment and a brooding quality can build up in the minds and souls of some thwarted Aries types, a tendency that you need to combat. Better by far to try and compromise, itself a word that doesn't exist in the vocabularies of the least enlightened people born under the sign of the Ram. Once this lesson is learned, inner happiness increases and you relax into your life much more.

The way you think about others is directly related to the way you consider they think about you. This leads to another surprising fact regarding the zodiac sign. Aries people absolutely hate to be disliked, though they would move heaven and earth to prove that this isn't the case. And as a result Aries both loves and hates with a passion. Deep inside you can sometimes be a child shivering in the dark. If you only realise this fact your path to happiness and success is almost assured. Of course to do so takes a good deal of courage – but that's a commodity you don't lack.

Making the best of yourself

It would be quite clear to any observer that you are not the sort of person who likes to hang around at the back of a queue, or who would relish constantly taking orders from people who may not know situations as well as you do. For that reason alone you are better in positions that see you out there at the front, giving commands and enjoying the cut and thrust of everyday life. In a career sense this means that whatever you do you are happiest telling those around you how to do it too. Many Aries people quite naturally find their way to the top of the tree and don't usually have too much trouble staying there.

It is important to remember, however, that there is another side to your nature: the giving qualities beneath your natural dominance. You can always be around when people need you the most, encouraging and even gently pushing when it is necessary. By keeping friends and being willing to nurture relationships across a broad spectrum, you gradually get to know what makes those around you tick. This makes for a more patient and understanding sort of Aries subject – the most potent of all.

Even your resilience is not endless, which is why it is important to remember that there are times when you need rest. Bearing in mind that you are not superhuman is the hardest lesson to learn, but the admission brings humility, something that Aries needs to cultivate whenever possible.

Try to avoid living a restricted life and make your social contacts frequent and important. Realise that there is much more to life than work and spend some of your free time genuinely attempting to help those who are less well off than you are. Crucially you must remember that 'help' is not the same as domination.

The impressions you give

This section may well be of less interest to Aries subjects than it would be to certain other zodiac signs. The reason is quite clear. Aries people are far less interested in what others think about them than almost anyone else – or at least they tell themselves that they are. Either way it is counterproductive to ignore the opinions of the world at large because to do so creates stumbling blocks, even in a practical sense.

Those around you probably find you extremely capable and well able to deal with almost any situation that comes your way. Most are willing to rely heavily on you and the majority would almost instinctively see you as a leader. Whether or not they like you at the same time is really dependent on the way you handle situations. That's the difference between the go-getting, sometimes selfish type of Aries subject and the more enlightened amongst this illustrious sign.

You are viewed as being exciting and well able to raise enthusiasm for almost any project that takes your fancy. Of course this implies a great responsibility because you are always expected to come up with the goods. The world tends to put certain people on a pedestal, and you are one of them. On the other side of the coin we are all inclined to fire arrows at the elevated, so maintaining your position isn't very easy.

Most of the time you are seen as being magnanimous and kind, factors that you can exploit, whilst at the same time recognising the depth of the responsibility that comes with being an Aries subject. It might not be a bad thing to allow those around you to see that you too have feet of clay. This will make them respect and support you all the more, and even Aries people really do need to feel loved. A well-balanced Aries subject is one of the most elevated spirits to be found anywhere.

The way forward

You certainly enjoy life more when looking at it from the top of the tree. Struggling to get by is not in the least interesting to your zodiac sign and you can soon become miserable if things are not going well for you. That's why it is probably quite justified in your case to work tenaciously in order to achieve your objectives. Ideally, once you have realised some sort of success and security for yourself, you should then be willing to sit and watch life go by a little more. In fact this doesn't happen. The reason for this is clear. The Aries subject who learns how to succeed rarely knows when to stop – it's as simple as that.

Splitting your life into different components can help, if only because this means that you don't get the various elements mixed up. So, for example, don't confuse your love life with your professional needs, or your family with colleagues. This process allows you to view life in manageable chunks and also makes it possible for you to realise when any one of them may be working well. As a result you will put the effort where it's needed, and enjoy what is going well for you.

If you want to know real happiness you will also have to learn that acquisition for its own sake brings hollow rewards at best. When your talents are being turned outward to the world at large, you are one of the most potent and successful people around. What is more you should find yourself to be a much happier person when you are lending a hand to the wider world. This is possible, maybe outside of your normal professional sphere, though even where voluntary work is concerned it is important not to push yourself to the point of fatigue.

Keep yourself physically fit, without necessarily expecting that you can run to the South Pole and back, and stay away from too many stimulants, such as alcohol and nicotine. The fact is that you are best when living a healthy life, but it doesn't help either if you make even abstinence into an art form. Balance is important, as is moderation – itself a word that is difficult for you to understand. In terms of your approach to other people it's important to realise that everyone has a specific point of view. These might be different to yours, but they are not necessarily wrong. Sort out the friends who are most important to you and stick with them, whilst at the same time realising that almost everyone can be a pal – with just a little effort.

14

ARIES ON THE CUSP

Astrological profiles are altered for those people born at either the beginning or the end of a zodiac sign, or, more properly, on the cusps of a sign. In the case of Aries this would be on the 21st of March and for two or three days after, and similarly at the end of the sign, probably from the 18th to the 20th of April.

The Pisces Cusp – March 21st to March 24th

With the Sun so close to the zodiac sign of Pisces at the time you were born, it is distinctly possible that you have always had some doubts when reading a character breakdown written specifically for the sign of Aries. This isn't surprising because no zodiac sign has a definite start or end, they merely merge together. As a result there are some of the characteristics of the sign of the Fishes that are intermingled with the qualities of Aries in your nature.

What we probably find, as a result, is a greater degree of emotional sensitivity and a tendency to be more cognisant of what the rest of humanity is feeling. This is not to imply that Aries is unfeeling, but rather that Pisceans actively make humanity their business.

You are still able to achieve your most desired objectives in the practical world, but on the way, you stop to listen to the heartbeat of the planet on which you live. A very good thing, of course, but at the same time there is some conflict created if your slightly dream-like tendencies get in the way of your absolute need to see things through to their logical conclusion.

Nobody knows you better than you know yourself, or at least that's what the Aries qualities within you say, but that isn't always verified by some of the self-doubt that comes from the direction of the Fishes. As in all matters astrological, a position of balance has to be achieved in order to reconcile the differing qualities of your nature. In your case, this is best accomplished by being willing to stop and think once in a while and by refusing to allow your depth to be a problem.

Dealt with properly, the conjoining of Pisces and Aries can be a wondrous and joyful affair, a harmony of opposites that always makes you interesting to know. Your position in the world is naturally one of authority but at the same time you need to serve. That's why some people with this sort of mixture of astrological qualities would make such good administrators in a hospital, or in any position where the alternate astrological needs are well balanced. In the chocolate box of life you are certainly a 'soft centre'.

The Taurus Cusp – April 18th to April 20th

The merge from Aries to Taurus is much less well defined than the one at the other side of Aries, but it can be very useful to you all the same. Like the Pisces-influenced Aries you may be slightly more quiet than would be the case with the Ram taken alone and your thought processes are probably not quite as fast. But to compensate for this fact you don't rush into things quite as much and are willing to allow ideas to mature more fully.

Your sense of harmony and beauty is strong and you know, in a very definite way, exactly what you want. As a result your home will be distinctive but tasteful and it's a place where you need space to be alone sometimes, which the true Aries subject probably does not. You do not lack the confidence to make things look the way you want them, but you have a need to display these things to the world at large and sometimes even to talk about how good you are at decoration and design.

If anyone finds you pushy, it is probably because they don't really know what makes you tick. Although you are willing to mix with almost anyone, you are more inclined, at base, to have a few very close friends who stay at the forefront of your life for a long time. It is likely that you enjoy refined company and you wouldn't take kindly to the dark, the sordid, or the downright crude in life.

Things don't get you down as much as can sometimes be seen to be the case for Taurus when taken alone and you are rarely stumped for a progressive and practical idea when one is needed most. At all levels, your creative energy is evident and some of you even have the ability to make this into a business, since Aries offers the practical and administrative spark that Taurus can sometimes lack.

In matters of love, you are ardent and sincere, probably an idealist, and you know what you want in a partner. Whilst this is also true in the case of Taurus, you are different, because you are much more likely, not only to look, but also to say something about the way you feel.

Being naturally friendly you rarely go short of the right sort of help and support when it is most vital. Part of the reason for this lies in the fact that you are so willing to be the sounding-board for the concerns of your friends. All in all you can be very contented with your lot, but you never stop searching for something better all the same. At its best, this is one of the most progressive cuspal matches of them all.

ARIES AND ITS ASCENDANTS

The nature of every individual on the planet is composed of the rich variety of zodiac signs and planetary positions that were present at the time of their birth. Your Sun sign, which in your case is Aries, is one of the many factors when it comes to assessing the unique person you are. Probably the most important consideration, other than your Sun sign, is to establish the zodiac sign that was rising over the eastern horizon at the time that you were born. This is your Ascending or Rising sign. Most popular astrology fails to take account of the Ascendant, and yet its importance remains with you from the very moment of your birth, through every day of your life. The Ascendant is evident in the way you approach the world, and so, when meeting a person for the first time, it is this astrological influence that you are most likely to notice first. Our Ascending sign essentially represents what we appear to be, while our Sun sign is what we feel inside ourselves.

The Ascendant also has the potential for modifying our overall nature. For example, if you were born at a time of day when Aries was passing over the eastern horizon (this would be around the time of dawn) then you would be classed as a double Aries. As such you would typify this zodiac sign, both internally and in your dealings with others. However, if your Ascendant sign turned out to be a Water sign, such as Pisces, there would be a profound alteration of nature, away from the expected qualities of Aries.

One of the reasons that popular astrology often ignores the Ascendant is that it has always been rather difficult to establish. We have found a way to make this possible by devising an easy-to-use table, which you will find on page 157 of this book. Using this, you can establish your Ascendant sign at a glance. You will need to know your rough time of birth, then it is simply a case of following the instructions.

For those readers who have no idea of their time of birth it might be worth allowing a good friend, or perhaps your partner, to read through the section that follows this introduction. Someone who deals with you on a regular basis may easily discover your Ascending sign, even though you could have some difficulty establishing it for yourself. A good understanding of this component of your nature is essential if you want to be aware of that 'other person' who is responsible for the way you make contact with the world at large. Your Sun sign, Ascendant sign, and the other pointers in this book will, together, allow you a far better understanding of what makes you tick as an individual. Peeling back the different layers of your astrological make-up can be an enlightening experience, and the Ascendant may represent one of the most important layers of all.

Aries with Aries Ascendant

What you see is what you get with this combination. You typify the no- nonsense approach of Aries at its best. All the same this combination is quite daunting when viewed through the eyes of other, less dominant sorts of people. You tend to push your way though situations that would find others cowering in a corner and you are afraid of very little. With a determination to succeed that makes you a force to be reckoned with, you leave the world in no doubt as to your intentions and tend to be rather too brusque for your own good on occasions.

At heart you are kind and loving, able to offer assistance to the downtrodden and sad, and usually willing to take on board the cares of people who have a part to play in your life. No-one would doubt your sincerity, or your honesty, though you may utilise slightly less than orthodox ways of getting your own way on those occasions when you feel you have right on your side. You are a loving partner and a good parent, though where children are concerned you tend to be rather too protective. The trouble is that you know what a big, bad world it can be and probably feel that you are better equipped to deal with things than anyone else.

Aries with Taurus Ascendant

This is a much quieter combination, so much so that even experienced astrologers would be unlikely to recognise you as an Aries subject at all, unless of course they came to know you very well. Your approach to life tends to be quiet and considered and there is a great danger that you could suppress those feelings that others of your kind would be only too willing to verbalise. To compensate you are deeply creative and will think matters through much more readily than more dominant Aries types would be inclined to do. Reaching out towards the world, you are, nevertheless, somewhat locked inside yourself and can struggle to achieve the level of communication that you so desperately need. Frustration might easily follow, were it not for the fact that you possess a quiet determination that, to those in the know, is the clearest window through to your Aries soul.

The care for others is stronger here than with almost any other Aries type and you certainly demonstrate this at all levels. The fact is that you live a great percentage of your life in service to the people you take to, whilst at the same time being able to shut the door firmly in the face of people who irritate or anger you. You are deeply motivated towards family relationships.

Aries with Gemini Ascendant

A fairly jolly combination this, though by no means easy for others to come to terms with. You fly about from pillar to post and rarely stop long enough to take a breath. Admittedly this suits your own needs very well, but it can be a source of some disquiet to those around you, since they may not possess your energy or motivation. Those who know you well are deeply in awe of your capacity to keep going long after almost everyone else would have given up and gone home, though this quality is not always as wonderful as it sounds because it means that you put more pressure on your nervous system than just about any other astrological combination. You need to be mindful of your nervous system, which responds to the erratic, mercurial quality of Gemini. Problems only really arise when the Aries part of you makes demands that the Gemini component finds difficult to deal with. There are paradoxes galore here and some of them need sorting out if you are ever fully to understand yourself, or are to be in a position when others know what makes you tick.

In relationships you might be a little fickle, but you are a real charmer and never stuck for the right words, no matter who you are dealing with. Your tenacity knows no bounds, though perhaps it should!

Aries with Cancer Ascendant

The main problem that you experience in life shows itself as a direct result of the meshing of these two very different zodiac signs. At heart Aries needs to dominate, whereas Cancer shows a desire to nurture. All too often the result can be a protective arm that is so strong that nobody could possibly get out from under it. Lighten your own load, and that of those you care for, by being willing to sit back and watch others please themselves a little. You might think that you know best, and your heart is clearly in the right place, but try to realise what life is like when someone is always on hand to tell you that they know better then you do.

But in a way this is a little severe, because you are fairly intuitive and your instincts would rarely lead you astray. Nobody could ask for a better partner or parent than you, though they might request a slightly less attentive one. In matters of work you are conscientious and are probably best suited to a job that means sorting out the kind of mess that humanity is so good at creating. You probably spend your spare time untangling balls of wool, though you are quite sporting too and could easily make the Olympics. Once there you would not win however, because you would be too concerned about all the other competitors.

Aries with Leo Ascendant

Here we come upon the first situation of Aries being allied with another Fire sign. This creates a character that could appear to be typically Aries at first sight and in many ways it is, though there are subtle differences that should not be ignored. Although you have the typical Aries ability to get things done, many of the tasks you do undertake will be for and on behalf of others. You can be proud, and on some occasions even haughty, and yet you are also regal in your bearing and honest to the point of absurdity. Nobody could doubt your sincerity and you have the soul of a poet combined with the courage of a lion.

All this is good, but it makes you rather difficult to approach, unless the person in question has first adopted a crouching and subservient attitude although you would not wish them to do so. It's simply that the impression you give and the motivation that underpins it are two quite different things. You are greatly respected and in the case of those individuals who know your real nature, you are also deeply loved. But life would be much simpler if you didn't always have to fight the wars that those around you are happy to start. Relaxation is a word that you don't really understand and you would do yourself a favour if you looked it up in a dictionary.

Aries with Virgo Ascendant

Virgo is steady and sure, though also fussy and stubborn. Aries is fast and determined, restless and active. It can already be seen that this is a rather strange meeting of characteristics and because Virgo is ruled by the capricious Mercury, the ultimate result will change from hour to hour and day to day. It isn't merely that others find it difficult to know where they are with you, they can't even understand what makes you tick. This will make you the subject of endless fascination and attention, at which you will be apparently surprised but inwardly pleased. If anyone ever really gets to know what goes on in that busy mind they may find the implications very difficult to deal with and it is a fact that only you would have the ability to live inside your crowded head.

As a partner and a parent you are second to none, though you tend to get on better with your children once they start to grow, since by this time you may be slightly less restricting to their own desires, which will often clash with your own on their behalf. You are capable of give and take and could certainly not be considered selfish, though your constant desire to get the best from everyone might occasionally be misconstrued.

Aries with Libra Ascendant

Libra has the tendency to bring out the best in any zodiac sign, and this is no exception when it comes together with Aries. You may, in fact, be the most comfortable of all Aries types, simply because Libra tempers some of your more assertive qualities and gives you the chance to balance out opposing forces, both inside yourself and in the world outside. You are fun to be with and make the staunchest friend possible. Although you are generally affable, few people would try to put one over on you, because they would quickly come to know how far you are willing to go before you let forth a string of invective that would shock those who previously underestimated your basic Aries traits.

Home and family are very dear to you, but you are more tolerant than some Aries types are inclined to be and you have a youthful zest for life that should stay with you no matter what age you manage to achieve. There is always something interesting to do and your mind is a constant stream of possibilities. This makes you very creative and you may also demonstrate a desire to look good at all times. You may not always be quite as confident as you appear to be, but few would guess the fact.

Aries with Scorpio Ascendant

The two very different faces of Mars come together in this potent, magnetic and quite awe-inspiring combination. Your natural inclination is towards secrecy and this fact, together with the natural attractions of the sensual Scorpio nature, makes you the object of great curiosity. This means that you will not go short of attention and should ensure that you are always being analysed by people who may never get to know you at all. At heart you prefer your own company, and yet life appears to find means to push you into the public gaze time and again. Most people with this combination ooze sex appeal and can use this fact as a stepping stone to personal success, yet without losing any integrity or loosening the cords of a deeply moralistic nature.

On those occasions when you do lose your temper, there isn't a character in the length and breadth of the zodiac who would have either the words or the courage to stand against the stream of invective that follows. On really rare occasions you might even scare yourself. As far as family members are concerned a simple look should be enough to show when you are not amused. Few people are left unmoved by your presence in their life.

Aries with Sagittarius Ascendant

What a lovely combination this can be, for the devil-may-care aspects of Sagittarius lighten the load of a sometimes too-serious Aries interior. Everything that glistens is not gold, though it's hard to convince you of the fact because, to mix metaphors, you can make a silk purse out of a sow's ear. Almost everyone loves you and in return you offer a friendship that is warm and protective, but not as demanding as sometimes tends to be the case with the Aries type. Relationships may be many and varied and there is often more than one major attachment in the life of those holding this combination. You will bring a breath of spring to any attachment, though you need to ensure that the person concerned is capable of keeping up with the hectic pace of your life.

It may appear from time to time that you are rather too trusting for your own good, though deep inside you are very astute and it seems that almost everything you undertake works out well in the end. This has nothing to do with native luck and is really down to the fact that you are much more calculating than might appear to be the case at first sight. As a parent you are protective yet offer sufficient room for self-expression.

Aries with Capricorn Ascendant

If ever anyone could be accused of setting off immediately, but slowly, it has to be you. These are very contradictory signs and the differences will express themselves in a variety of ways. One thing is certain, you have tremendous tenacity and will see a job through patiently from beginning to end, without tiring on the way, and ensuring that every detail is taken care of properly. This combination often bestows good health and a great capacity for continuity, particularly in terms of the length of life. You are certainly not as argumentative as the typical Aries, but you do know how to get your own way, which is just as well because you are usually thinking on behalf of everyone else and not just on your own account.

At home you can relax, which is a blessing for Aries, though in fact you seldom choose to do so because you always have some project or other on the go. You probably enjoy knocking down and rebuilding walls, though this is a practical tendency and not responsive to relationships, in which you are ardent and sincere. Impetuosity is as close to your heart as is the case for any type of Aries subject, though you certainly have the ability to appear patient and steady. But it's just a front, isn't it?

Aries with Aquarius Ascendant

The person standing on a soap box in the corner of the park, extolling the virtues of this or that, could quite easily be an Aries with an Aquarian Ascendant. You are certainly not averse to speaking your mind and you have plenty to talk about because you are the best social reformer and political animal of them all. Unorthodox in your approach, you have the ability to keep everyone guessing, except when it comes to getting your own way, for in this nobody doubts your natural abilities. You can put theories into practice very well and on the way you retain a sense of individuality that would shock more conservative types. It's true that a few people might find you a little difficult to approach and this is partly because you have an inner reserve and strength which is difficult forothers to fathom.

In the world at large you take your place at the front, as any good Arian should, and yet you offer room for others to share your platform. You keep up with the latest innovations and treat family members as the genuine friends that you believe them to be. Care needs to be taken when picking a life partner, for you are an original, and not just anyone could match the peculiarities thrown up by this astrological combination.

Aries with Pisces Ascendant

Although not an easy combination to deal with, the Aries with a Piscean Ascendant does, nevertheless, bring something very special to the world in the way of natural understanding allied to practical assistance. It's true that you can sometimes be a dreamer, but there is nothing wrong with that as long as you have the ability to turn some of your wishes into reality, and this you are easily able to do, usually for the sake of those around you. Conversation comes easily to you, though you also possess a slightly wistful and poetic side to your nature, which is attractive to the many people who call you a friend. A natural entertainer, you bring a sense of the comic to the often serious qualities of Aries, though without losing the determination that typifies the sign.

In relationships you are ardent, sincere and supportive, with a strong social conscience that sometimes finds you fighting the battles of the less privileged members of society. Family is important to you and this is a combination that invariably leads to parenthood. Away from the cut and thrust of everyday life you relax more fully and think about matters more deeply than more typical Aries types might.

THE MOON AND THE PART IT PLAYS IN YOUR LIFE

In astrology the Moon is probably the single most important heavenly body after the Sun. Its unique position, as partner to the Earth on its journey around the solar system, means that the Moon appears to pass through the signs of the zodiac extremely quickly. The zodiac position of the Moon at the time of your birth plays a great part in personal character and is especially significant in the build-up of your emotional nature.

Your Own Moon Sign

Discovering the position of the Moon at the time of your birth has always been notoriously difficult because tracking the complex zodiac positions of the Moon is not easy. This process has been reduced to three simple stages with our Lunar Tables. A breakdown of the Moon's zodiac positions can be found from page 35 onwards, so that once you know what your Moon Sign is, you can see what part this plays in the overall build-up of your personal character.

If you follow the instructions on the next page you will soon be able to work out exactly what zodiac sign the Moon occupied on the day that you were born and you can then go on to compare the reading for this position with those of your Sun sign and your Ascendant. It is partly the comparison between these three important positions that goes towards making you the unique individual you are.

HOW TO DISCOVER YOUR MOON SIGN

This is a three-stage process. You may need a pen and a piece of paper but if you follow the instructions below the process should only take a minute or so.

STAGE 1 First of all you need to know the Moon Age at the time of your birth. If you look at Moon Table 1, on page 33, you will find all the years between 1910 and 2008 down the left side. Find the year of your birth and then trace across to the right to the month of your birth. Where the two intersect you will find a number. This is the date of the New Moon in the month that you were born. You now need to count forward the number of days between the New Moon and your own birthday. For example, if the New Moon in the month of your birth was shown as being the 6th and you were born on the 20th, your Moon Age Day would be 14. If the New Moon in the month of your birth came after your birthday, you need to count forward from the New Moon in the previous month. If you were born in a Leap Year, remember to count the 29th February. You can tell if your birth year was a Leap Year if the last two digits can be divided by four. Whatever the result, jot this number down so that you do not forget it.

STAGE 2 Take a look at Moon Table 2 on page 34. Down the left hand column look for the date of your birth. Now trace across to the month of your birth. Where the two meet you will find a letter. Copy this letter down alongside your Moon Age Day.

STAGE 3 Moon Table 3 on page 34 will supply you with the zodiac sign the Moon occupied on the day of your birth. Look for your Moon Age Day down the left hand column and then for the letter you found in Stage 2. Where the two converge you will find a zodiac sign and this is the sign occupied by the Moon on the day that you were born.

Your Zodiac Moon Sign Explained

You will find a profile of all zodiac Moon Signs on pages 35 to 38, showing in yet another way how astrology helps to make you into the individual that you are. In each daily entry of the Astral Diary you can find the zodiac position of the Moon for every day of the year. This also allows you to discover your lunar birthdays. Since the Moon passes through all the signs of the zodiac in about a month, you can expect something like twelve lunar birthdays each year. At these times you are likely to be emotionally steady and able to make the sort of decisions that have real, lasting value.

MOON TABLE 1

YEAR	FEB	MAR	APR	YEAR	FEB	MAR	APR	YEAR	FEB	MAR	APR
1910	9	11	9	1943	4	6	4	1976	29	30	29
1911	28	30	28	1944	24	24	22	1977	18	19	18
1912	17	19	18	1945	12	14	12	1978	7	9	7
1913	6	7	6	1946	2	3	2	1979	26	27	26
1914	24	26	24	1947	19	21	20	1980	15	16	15
1915	14	15	13	1948	9	11	9	1981	4	6	4
1916	3	5	3	1949	27	29	28	1982	23	24	23
1917	22	23	22	1950	16	18	17	1983	13	14	13
1918	11	12	11	1951	6	7	6	1984	1	2	1
1919	–	2/31	30	1952	25	25	24	1985	19	21	20
1920	19	20	18	1953	14	15	13	1986	9	10	9
1921	8	9	8	1954	3	5	3	1987	28	29	28
1922	26	28	27	1955	22	24	22	1988	17	18	16
1923	15	17	16	1956	11	12	11	1989	6	7	6
1924	5	5	4	1957	–	1/31	29	1990	25	26	25
1925	23	24	23	1958	18	20	19	1991	14	15	13
1926	12	14	12	1959	7	9	8	1992	3	4	3
1927	2	3	2	1960	26	27	26	1993	22	24	22
1928	19	21	20	1961	15	16	15	1994	10	12	11
1929	9	11	9	1962	5	6	5	1995	29	30	29
1930	28	30	28	1963	23	25	23	1996	18	19	18
1931	17	19	18	1964	13	14	12	1997	7	9	7
1932	6	7	6	1965	1	2	1	1998	26	27	26
1933	24	26	24	1966	19	21	20	1999	16	17	16
1934	14	15	13	1967	9	10	9	2000	5	6	4
1935	3	5	3	1968	28	29	28	2001	23	24	23
1936	22	23	21	1969	17	18	16	2002	12	13	12
1937	11	13	12	1970	6	7	6	2003	–	2	1
1938	–	2/31	30	1971	25	26	25	2004	20	21	19
1939	19	20	19	1972	14	15	13	2005	9	10	8
1940	8	9	7	1973	4	5	3	2006	28	29	27
1941	26	27	26	1974	22	24	22	2007	15	18	17
1942	15	16	15	1975	11	12	11	2008	6	7	6

TABLE 2 MOON TABLE 3

DAY	MAR	APR	M/D	F	G	H	I	J	K	L
1	F	J	0	PI	PI	AR	AR	AR	TA	TA
2	G	J	1	PI	AR	AR	AR	TA	TA	TA
3	G	J	2	AR	AR	AR	TA	TA	TA	GE
4	G	J	3	AR	AR	TA	TA	TA	GE	GE
5	G	J	4	AR	TA	TA	GE	GE	GE	GE
6	G	J	5	TA	TA	GE	GE	GE	CA	CA
7	G	J	6	TA	GE	GE	GE	CA	CA	CA
8	G	J	7	GE	GE	GE	CA	CA	CA	LE
9	G	J	8	GE	GE	CA	CA	CA	LE	LE
10	G	J	9	CA	CA	CA	CA	LE	LE	VI
11	G	K	10	CA	CA	LE	LE	LE	VI	VI
12	H	K	11	CA	LE	LE	LE	VI	VI	VI
13	H	K	12	LE	LE	LE	VI	VI	VI	LI
14	H	K	13	LE	LE	VI	VI	VI	LI	LI
15	H	K	14	VI	VI	VI	LI	LI	LI	LI
16	H	K	15	VI	VI	LI	LI	LI	SC	SC
17	H	K	16	VI	LI	LI	LI	SC	SC	SC
18	H	K	17	LI	LI	LI	SC	SC	SC	SA
19	H	K	18	LI	LI	SC	SC	SC	SA	SA
20	H	K	19	LI	SC	SC	SC	SA	SA	SA
21	H	L	20	SC	SC	SA	SA	SA	CP	CP
22	I	L	21	SC	SA	SA	SA	CP	CP	CP
23	I	L	22	SC	SA	SA	CP	CP	CP	AQ
24	I	L	23	SA	SA	CP	CP	CP	AQ	AQ
25	I	L	24	SA	CP	CP	CP	AQ	AQ	AQ
26	I	L	25	CP	CP	AQ	AQ	AQ	PI	PI
27	I	L	26	CP	AQ	AQ	AQ	PI	PI	PI
28	I	L	27	AQ	AQ	AQ	PI	PI	PI	AR
29	I	L	28	AQ	AQ	PI	PI	PI	AR	AR
30	I	L	29	AQ	PI	PI	PI	AR	AR	AR
31	I	–								

AR = Aries, TA = Taurus, GE = Gemini, CA = Cancer, LE = Leo, VI = Virgo, LI = Libra, SC = Scorpio, SA = Sagittarius, CP = Capricorn, AQ = Aquarius, PI = Pisces

MOON SIGNS

Moon in Aries

You have a strong imagination, courage, determination and a desire to do things in your own way and forge your own path through life.

Originality is a key attribute; you are seldom stuck for ideas although your mind is changeable and you could take the time to focus on individual tasks. Often quick-tempered, you take orders from few people and live life at a fast pace. Avoid health problems by taking regular time out for rest and relaxation.

Emotionally, it is important that you talk to those you are closest to and work out your true feelings. Once you discover that people are there to help, there is less necessity for you to do everything yourself.

Moon in Taurus

The Moon in Taurus gives you a courteous and friendly manner, which means you are likely to have many friends.

The good things in life mean a lot to you, as Taurus is an Earth sign that delights in experiences which please the senses. Hence you are probably a lover of good food and drink, which may in turn mean you need to keep an eye on the bathroom scales, especially as looking good is also important to you.

Emotionally you are fairly stable and you stick by your own standards. Taureans do not respond well to change. Intuition also plays an important part in your life.

Moon in Gemini

You have a warm-hearted character, sympathetic and eager to help others. At times reserved, you can also be articulate and chatty: this is part of the paradox of Gemini, which always brings duplicity to the nature. You are interested in current affairs, have a good intellect, and are good company and likely to have many friends. Most of your friends have a high opinion of you and would be ready to defend you should the need arise. However, this is usually unnecessary, as you are quite capable of defending yourself in any verbal confrontation.

Travel is important to your inquisitive mind and you find intellectual stimulus in mixing with people from different cultures. You also gain much from reading, writing and the arts but you do need plenty of rest and relaxation in order to avoid fatigue.

Moon in Cancer

The Moon in Cancer at the time of birth is a fortunate position as Cancer is the Moon's natural home. This means that the qualities of compassion and understanding given by the Moon are especially enhanced in your nature, and you are friendly and sociable and cope well with emotional pressures. You cherish home and family life, and happily do the domestic tasks. Your surroundings are important to you and you hate squalor and filth. You are likely to have a love of music and poetry.

Your basic character, although at times changeable like the Moon itself, depends on symmetry. You aim to make your surroundings comfortable and harmonious, for yourself and those close to you.

Moon in Leo

The best qualities of the Moon and Leo come together to make you warm-hearted, fair, ambitious and self-confident. With good organisational abilities, you invariably rise to a position of responsibility in your chosen career. This is fortunate as you don't enjoy being an 'also-ran' and would rather be an important part of a small organisation than a menial in a large one.

You should be lucky in love, and happy, provided you put in the effort to make a comfortable home for yourself and those close to you. It is likely that you will have a love of pleasure, sport, music and literature. Life brings you many rewards, most of them as a direct result of your own efforts, although you may be luckier than average and ready to make the best of any situation.

Moon in Virgo

You are endowed with good mental abilities and a keen receptive memory, but you are never ostentatious or pretentious. Naturally quite reserved, you still have many friends, especially of the opposite sex. Marital relationships must be discussed carefully and worked at so that they remain harmonious, as personal attachments can be a problem if you do not give them your full attention.

Talented and persevering, you possess artistic qualities and are a good homemaker. Earning your honours through genuine merit, you work long and hard towards your objectives but show little pride in your achievements. Many short journeys will be undertaken in your life.

Moon in Libra

With the Moon in Libra you are naturally popular and make friends easily. People like you, probably more than you realise, you bring fun to a party and are a natural diplomat. For all its good points, Libra is not the most stable of astrological signs and, as a result, your emotions can be a little unstable too. Therefore, although the Moon in Libra is said to be good for love and marriage, your Sun sign and Rising sign will have an important effect on your emotional and loving qualities.

You must remember to relate to others in your decision-making. Co-operation is crucial because Libra represents the 'balance' of life that can only be achieved through harmonious relationships. Conformity is not easy for you because Libra, an Air sign, likes its independence.

Moon in Scorpio

Some people might call you pushy. In fact, all you really want to do is to live life to the full and protect yourself and your family from the pressures of life. Take care to avoid giving the impression of being sarcastic or impulsive and use your energies wisely and constructively.

You have great courage and you invariably achieve your goals by force of personality and sheer effort. You are fond of mystery and are good at predicting the outcome of situations and events. Travel experiences can be beneficial to you.

You may experience problems if you do not take time to examine your motives in a relationship, and also if you allow jealousy, always a feature of Scorpio, to cloud your judgement.

Moon in Sagittarius

The Moon in Sagittarius helps to make you a generous individual with humanitarian qualities and a kind heart. Restlessness may be intrinsic as your mind is seldom still. Perhaps because of this, you have a need for change that could lead you to several major moves during your adult life. You are not afraid to stand your ground when you know your judgement is right, you speak directly and have good intuition.

At work you are quick, efficient and versatile and so you make an ideal employee. You need work to be intellectually demanding and do not enjoy tedious routines.

In relationships, you anger quickly if faced with stupidity or deception, though you are just as quick to forgive and forget. Emotionally, there are times when your heart rules your head.

Moon in Capricorn

The Moon in Capricorn makes you popular and likely to come into the public eye in some way. The watery Moon is not entirely comfortable in the Earth sign of Capricorn and this may lead to some difficulties in the early years of life. An initial lack of creative ability and indecision must be overcome before the true qualities of patience and perseverance inherent in Capricorn can show through.

You have good administrative ability and are a capable worker, and if you are careful you can accumulate wealth. But you must be cautious and take professional advice in partnerships, as you are open to deception. You may be interested in social or welfare work, which suit your organisational skills and sympathy for others.

Moon in Aquarius

The Moon in Aquarius makes you an active and agreeable person with a friendly, easy-going nature. Sympathetic to the needs of others, you flourish in a laid-back atmosphere. You are broad-minded, fair and open to suggestion, although sometimes you have an unconventional quality which others can find hard to understand.

You are interested in the strange and curious, and in old articles and places. You enjoy trips to these places and gain much from them. Political, scientific and educational work interests you and you might choose a career in science or technology.

Money-wise, you make gains through innovation and concentration and Lunar Aquarians often tackle more than one job at a time. In love you are kind and honest.

Moon in Pisces

You have a kind, sympathetic nature, somewhat retiring at times, but you always take account of others' feelings and help when you can.

Personal relationships may be problematic, but as life goes on you can learn from your experiences and develop a better understanding of yourself and the world around you.

You have a fondness for travel, appreciate beauty and harmony and hate disorder and strife. You may be fond of literature and would make a good writer or speaker yourself. You have a creative imagination and may come across as an incurable romantic. You have strong intuition, maybe bordering on a mediumistic quality, which sets you apart from the mass. You may not be rich in cash terms, but your personal gifts are worth more than gold.

ARIES IN LOVE

Discover how compatible in love you are with people from the same and other signs of the zodiac. Five stars equals a match made in heaven!

Aries meets Aries

This could be be an all-or-nothing pairing. Both parties are from a dominant sign, so someone will have to be flexible in order to maintain personal harmony. Both know what they want out of life, and may have trouble overcoming any obstacles a relationship creates. This is a good physical pairing, with a chemistry that few other matches enjoy to the same level. Attitude is everything, but at least there is a mutual admiration that makes gazing at your partner like looking in the mirror. Star rating: ****

Aries meets Taurus

This is a match that has been known to work very well. Aries brings dynamism and ambition, while Taurus has the patience to see things through logically. Such complementary views work equally well in a relationship or in the office. There is mutual respect, but sometimes a lack of total understanding. The romantic needs of each are quite different, but both are still fulfilled. They can live easily in domestic harmony which is very important but, interestingly, Aries may be the loser in battles of will. Star rating: ***

Aries meets Gemini

Don't expect peace and harmony with this combination, although what comes along instead might make up for any disagreements. Gemini has a very fertile imagination, while Aries has the tenacity to make reality from fantasy. Combined, they have a sizzling relationship. There are times when both parties could explode with indignation and something has to give. But even if there are clashes, making them up will always be most enjoyable! Mutual financial success is likely in this match. Star rating: ****

Aries meets Cancer

A potentially one-sided pairing, it often appears that the Cancerian is brow-beaten by the far more dominant Arian. So much depends on the patience of the Cancerian individual, because if good psychology is present – who knows? But beware, Aries, you may find your partner too passive, and constantly having to take the lead can be wearing – even for you. A prolonged trial period would be advantageous, as the match could easily go either way. When it does work, though, this relationship is usually contented. Star rating: ***

Aries meets Leo

Stand by for action and make sure the house is sound-proof. Leo is a lofty idealist and there is always likely to be friction when two Fire signs meet. To compensate, there is much mutual admiration, together with a desire to please. Where there are shared incentives, the prognosis is good but it's important not to let little irritations blow up. Both signs want to have their own way and this is a sure cause of trouble. There might not be much patience here, but there is plenty of action. Star rating: *****

Aries meets Virgo

Neither of these signs really understands the other, and that could easily lead to a clash. Virgo is so pedantic, which will drive Aries up the wall, while Aries always wants to be moving on to the next objective, before Virgo is even settled with the last one. It will take time for these two to get to know each other, but this is a great business matching. If a personal relationship is seen in these terms then the prognosis can be good, but on the whole, this is not an inspiring match. Star rating: ***

Aries meets Libra

These signs are zodiac opposites which means a make-or-break situation. The match will either be a great success or a dismal failure. Why? Well Aries finds it difficult to understand the flighty Air-sign tendencies of Libra, whilst the natural balance of Libra contradicts the unorthodox Arian methods. Any flexibility will come from Libra, which may mean that things work out for a while, but Libra only has so much patience and it may eventually run out. In the end, Aries may be just too bossy for an independent but sensitive sign like Libra. Star rating: **

Aries meets Scorpio

There can be great affection here, even if the two zodiac signs are so very different. The common link is the planet Mars, which plays a part in both these natures. Although Aries is, outwardly, the most dominant, Scorpio people are among the most powerful to be found anywhere. This quiet determination is respected by Aries. Aries will satisfy the passionate side of Scorpio, particularly with instruction from Scorpio. There are mysteries here which will add spice to life. The few arguments that do occur are likely to be awe-inspiring. Star rating: ****

Aries meets Sagittarius

This can be one of the most favourable matches of them all. Both Aries and Sagittarius are Fire signs, which often leads to clashes of will, but this pair find a mutual understanding. Sagittarius helps Aries to develop a better sense of humour, while Aries teaches the Archer about consistency on the road to success. Some patience is called for on both sides, but these people have a natural liking for each other. Add this to growing love and you have a long-lasting combination that is hard to beat. Star rating: *****

Aries meets Capricorn

Capricorn works conscientiously to achieve its objectives and so can be the perfect companion for Aries. The Ram knows how to achieve but not how to consolidate, so the two signs have a great deal to offer one another practically. There may not be fireworks and it's sometimes doubtful how well they know each other, but it may not matter. Aries is outwardly hot but inwardly cool, whilst Capricorn can appear low key but be a furnace underneath. Such a pairing can gradually find contentment, though both parties may wonder how this is so. Star rating: ****

Aries meets Aquarius

Aquarius is an Air sign, and Air and Fire often work well together, but perhaps not in the case of Aries and Aquarius. The average Aquarian lives in what the Ram sees as a fantasy world, so without a sufficiently good meeting of minds, compromise may be lacking. Of course, almost anything is possible, and the dominant side of Aries could be trained by the devil-may-care attitude of Aquarius. There are meeting points but they are difficult to establish. However, given sufficient time and an open mind on both sides, a degree of happiness is possible. Star rating: **

Aries meets Pisces

Still waters run deep, and they don't come much deeper than Pisces. Although these signs share the same quadrant of the zodiac, they have little in common. Pisces is a dreamer, a romantic idealist with steady and spiritual goals. Aries needs to be on the move, and has very different ideals. It's hard to see how a relationship could develop because the outlook on life is so different but, with patience, especially from Aries, there is a chance that things might work out. Pisces needs incentive, and Aries may be the sign to offer it. Star rating: **

VENUS:
THE PLANET OF LOVE

If you look up at the sky around sunset or sunrise you will often see Venus in close attendance to the Sun. It is arguably one of the most beautiful sights of all and there is little wonder that historically it became associated with the goddess of love. But although Venus does play an important part in the way you view love and in the way others see you romantically, this is only one of the spheres of influence that it enjoys in your overall character.

Venus has a part to play in the more cultured side of your life and has much to do with your appreciation of art, literature, music and general creativity. Even the way you look is responsive to the part of the zodiac that Venus occupied at the start of your life, though this fact is also down to your Sun sign and Ascending sign. If, at the time you were born, Venus occupied one of the more gregarious zodiac signs, you will be more likely to wear your heart on your sleeve, as well as to be more attracted to entertainment, social gatherings and good company. If on the other hand Venus occupied a quiet zodiac sign at the time of your birth, you would tend to be more retiring and less willing to shine in public situations.

It's good to know what part the planet Venus plays in your life for it can have a great bearing on the way you appear to the rest of the world and since we all have to mix with others, you can learn to make the very best of what Venus has to offer you.

One of the great complications in the past has always been trying to establish exactly what zodiac position Venus enjoyed when you were born because the planet is notoriously difficult to track. However, we have solved that problem by creating a table that is exclusive to your Sun sign, which you will find on the following page.

Establishing your Venus sign could not be easier. Just look up the year of your birth on the following page and you will see a sign of the zodiac. This was the sign that Venus occupied in the period covered by your sign in that year. If Venus occupied more than one sign during the period, this is indicated by the date on which the sign changed, and the name of the new sign. For instance, if you were born in 1950, Venus was in Aquarius until the 7th April, after which time it was in Pisces. If you were born before 7th April your Venus sign is Aquarius, if you were born on or after 7th April, your Venus sign is Pisces. Once you have established the position of Venus at the time of your birth, you can then look in the pages which follow to see how this has a bearing on your life as a whole.

1910 AQUARIUS / 5.4 PISCES
1911 ARIES / 25.3 TAURUS
1912 PISCES / 14.4 ARIES
1913 TAURUS
1914 ARIES /14.4 TAURUS
1915 AQUARIUS / 1.4 PISCES
1916 TAURUS / 8.4 GEMINI
1917 PISCES / 28.3 ARIES
1918 AQUARIUS / 5.4 PISCES
1919 ARIES / 24.3 TAURUS
1920 PISCES / 14.4 ARIES
1921 TAURUS
1922 ARIES / 13.4 TAURUS
1923 AQUARIUS / 1.4 PISCES
1924 TAURUS / 6.4 GEMINI
1925 PISCES / 28.3 ARIES
1926 AQUARIUS / 6.4 PISCES
1927 ARIES / 24.3 TAURUS
1928 PISCES / 13.4 ARIES
1929 TAURUS / 20.4 ARIES
1930 ARIES / 13.4 TAURUS
1931 AQUARIUS / 31.3 PISCES
1932 TAURUS / 6.4 GEMINI
1933 PISCES / 27.3 ARIES
1934 AQUARIUS / 6.4 PISCES
1935 ARIES / 23.3 TAURUS
1936 PISCES / 13.4 ARIES
1937 TAURUS / 14.4 ARIES
1938 ARIES / 12.4 TAURUS
1939 AQUARIUS / 31.3 PISCES
1940 TAURUS / 5.4 GEMINI
1941 PISCES / 26.3 ARIES /
    20.4 TAURUS
1942 AQUARIUS / 7.4 PISCES
1943 ARIES / 23.3 TAURUS
1944 PISCES / 12.4 ARIES
1945 TAURUS / 8.4 ARIES
1946 ARIES / 12.4 TAURUS
1947 AQUARIUS / 30.3 PISCES
1948 TAURUS / 5.4 GEMINI
1949 PISCES / 25.3 ARIES /
    20.4 TAURUS
1950 AQUARIUS / 7.4 PISCES
1951 ARIES / 22.3 TAURUS
1952 PISCES / 12.4 ARIES
1953 TAURUS / 1.4 ARIES
1954 ARIES / 11.4 TAURUS
1955 AQUARIUS / 30.3 PISCES
1956 TAURUS / 4.4 GEMINI
1957 PISCES / 25.3 ARIES /
    19.4 TAURUS
1958 AQUARIUS / 8.4 PISCES
1959 ARIES / 22.3 TAURUS
1960 PISCES / 11.4 ARIES

1961 ARIES
1962 ARIES / 11.4 TAURUS
1963 AQUARIUS / 29.3 PISCES
1964 TAURUS / 4.4 GEMINI
1965 PISCES / 24.3 ARIES /
    19.4 TAURUS
1966 AQUARIUS / 8.4 PISCES
1967 TAURUS / 20.4 GEMINI
1968 PISCES / 10.4 ARIES
1969 ARIES
1970 ARIES / 10.4 TAURUS
1971 AQUARIUS / 29.3 PISCES
1972 TAURUS / 3.4 GEMINI
1973 PISCES / 24.3 ARIES /
    18.4 TAURUS
1974 AQUARIUS / 8.4 PISCES
1975 TAURUS / 19.4 GEMINI
1976 PISCES / 10.4 ARIES
1977 ARIES
1978 ARIES / 10.4 TAURUS
1979 AQUARIUS / 28.3 PISCES
1980 TAURUS / 3.4 GEMINI
1981 PISCES / 23.3 ARIES /
    18.4 TAURUS
1982 AQUARIUS / 9.4 PISCES
1983 TAURUS / 19.4 GEMINI
1984 PISCES / 9.4 ARIES
1985 ARIES
1986 ARIES / 9.4 TAURUS
1987 AQUARIUS / 28.3 PISCES
1988 TAURUS / 2.4 GEMINI
1989 PISCES / 23.3 ARIES /
    17.4 TAURUS
1990 AQUARIUS / 9.4 PISCES
1991 TAURUS / 18.4 GEMINI
1992 PISCES / 9.4 ARIES
1993 ARIES
1994 ARIES / 9.4 TAURUS
1995 AQUARIUS / 27.3 PISCES
1996 TAURUS / 2.4 GEMINI
1997 PISCES / 22.3 ARIES /
    17.4 TAURUS
1998 AQUARIUS / 9.4 PISCES
1999 TAURUS / 18.4 GEMINI
2000 PISCES / 9.4 ARIES
2001 ARIES
2002 ARIES / 7.4 TAURUS
2003 AQUARIUS / 27.3 PISCES
2004 TAURUS / 1.4 GEMINI
2005 PISCES/22.3 ARIES
2006 AQUARIUS/7.4 PISCES
2007 TAURUS / 16.4 GEMINI
2008 PISCES / 9.4 ARIES

44

VENUS THROUGH THE ZODIAC SIGNS

Venus in Aries

Amongst other things, the position of Venus in Aries indicates a fondness for travel, music and all creative pursuits. Your nature tends to be affectionate and you would try not to create confusion or difficulty for others if it could be avoided. Many people with this planetary position have a great love of the theatre, and mental stimulation is of the greatest importance. Early romantic attachments are common with Venus in Aries, so it is very important to establish a genuine sense of romantic continuity. Early marriage is not recommended, especially if it is based on sympathy. You may give your heart a little too readily on occasions.

Venus in Taurus

You are capable of very deep feelings and your emotions tend to last for a very long time. This makes you a trusting partner and lover, whose constancy is second to none. In life you are precise and careful and always try to do things the right way. Although this means an ordered life, which you are comfortable with, it can also lead you to be rather too fussy for your own good. Despite your pleasant nature, you are very fixed in your opinions and quite able to speak your mind. Others are attracted to you and historical astrologers always quoted this position of Venus as being very fortunate in terms of marriage. However, if you find yourself involved in a failed relationship, it could take you a long time to trust again.

Venus in Gemini

As with all associations related to Gemini, you tend to be quite versatile, anxious for change and intelligent in your dealings with the world at large. You may gain money from more than one source but you are equally good at spending it. There is an inference here that you are a good communicator, via either the written or the spoken word, and you love to be in the company of interesting people. Always on the look-out for culture, you may also be very fond of music, and love to indulge the curious and cultured side of your nature. In romance you tend to have more than one relationship and could find yourself associated with someone who has previously been a friend or even a distant relative.

Venus in Cancer

You often stay close to home because you are very fond of family and enjoy many of your most treasured moments when you are with those you love. Being naturally sympathetic, you will always do anything you can to support those around you, even people you hardly know at all. This charitable side of your nature is your most noticeable trait and is one of the reasons why others are naturally so fond of you. Being receptive and in some cases even psychic, you can see through to the soul of most of those with whom you come into contact. You may not commence too many romantic attachments but when you do give your heart, it tends to be unconditionally.

Venus in Leo

It must become quickly obvious to almost anyone you meet that you are kind, sympathetic and yet determined enough to stand up for anyone or anything that is truly important to you. Bright and sunny, you warm the world with your natural enthusiasm and would rarely do anything to hurt those around you, or at least not intentionally. In romance you are ardent and sincere, though some may find your style just a little overpowering. Gains come through your contacts with other people and this could be especially true with regard to romance, for love and money often come hand in hand for those who were born with Venus in Leo. People claim to understand you, though you are more complex than you seem.

Venus in Virgo

Your nature could well be fairly quiet no matter what your Sun sign might be, though this fact often manifests itself as an inner peace and would not prevent you from being basically sociable. Some delays and even the odd disappointment in love cannot be ruled out with this planetary position, though it's a fact that you will usually find the happiness you look for in the end. Catapulting yourself into romantic entanglements that you know to be rather ill-advised is not sensible, and it would be better to wait before you committed yourself exclusively to any one person. It is the essence of your nature to serve the world at large and through doing so it is possible that you will attract money at some stage in your life.

Venus in Libra

Venus is very comfortable in Libra and bestows upon those people who have this planetary position a particular sort of kindness that is easy to recognise. This is a very good position for all sorts of friendships and also for romantic attachments that usually bring much joy into your life. Few individuals with Venus in Libra would avoid marriage and since you are capable of great depths of love, it is likely that you will find a contented personal life. You like to mix with people of integrity and intelligence but don't take kindly to scruffy surroundings or work that means getting your hands too dirty. Careful speculation, good business dealings and money through marriage all seem fairly likely.

Venus in Scorpio

You are quite open and tend to spend money quite freely, even on those occasions when you don't have very much. Although your intentions are always good, there are times when you get yourself in to the odd scrape and this can be particularly true when it comes to romance, which you may come to late or from a rather unexpected direction. Certainly you have the power to be happy and to make others contented on the way, but you find the odd stumbling block on your journey through life and it could seem that you have to work harder than those around you. As a result of this, you gain a much deeper understanding of the true value of personal happiness than many people ever do, and are likely to achieve true contentment in the end.

Venus in Sagittarius

You are lighthearted, cheerful and always able to see the funny side of any situation. These facts enhance your popularity, which is especially high with members of the opposite sex. You should never have to look too far to find romantic interest in your life, though it is just possible that you might be too willing to commit yourself before you are certain that the person in question is right for you. Part of the problem here extends to other areas of life too. The fact is that you like variety in everything and so can tire of situations that fail to offer it. All the same, if you choose wisely and learn to understand your restless side, then great happiness can be yours.

47

Venus in Capricorn

The most notable trait that comes from Venus in this position is that it makes you trustworthy and able to take on all sorts of responsibilities in life. People are instinctively fond of you and love you all the more because you are always ready to help those who are in any form of need. Social and business popularity can be yours and there is a magnetic quality to your nature that is particularly attractive in a romantic sense. Anyone who wants a partner for a lover, a spouse and a good friend too would almost certainly look in your direction. Constancy is the hallmark of your nature and unfaithfulness would go right against the grain. You might sometimes be a little too trusting.

Venus in Aquarius

This location of Venus offers a fondness for travel and a desire to try out something new at every possible opportunity. You are extremely easy to get along with and tend to have many friends from varied backgrounds, classes and inclinations. You like to live a distinct sort of life and gain a great deal from moving about, both in a career sense and with regard to your home. It is not out of the question that you could form a romantic attachment to someone who comes from far away or be attracted to a person of a distinctly artistic and original nature. What you cannot stand is jealousy, for you have friends of both sexes and would want to keep things that way.

Venus in Pisces

The first thing people tend to notice about you is your wonderful, warm smile. Being very charitable by nature you will do anything to help others, even if you don't know them well. Much of your life may be spent sorting out situations for other people, but it is very important to feel that you are living for yourself too. In the main, you remain cheerful, and tend to be quite attractive to members of the opposite sex. Where romantic attachments are concerned, you could be drawn to people who are significantly older or younger than yourself or to someone with a unique career or point of view. It might be best for you to avoid marrying whilst you are still very young.

ARIES:
2007 DIARY PAGES

October

2007

1 MONDAY
Moon Age Day 19   Moon Sign Gemini

It's the first day of a new month and you have a chance to make a really good impression on someone you see as being very significant. Don't go at things like a bull at a gate but show a degree of ingenuity and allow matters to develop slowly. It's a little like catching a fish. Rushing probably doesn't help.

2 TUESDAY
Moon Age Day 20   Moon Sign Gemini

You have what it takes to make yourself popular with others today and this really is the key to success for most Aries people around this time. Attitude is very important in professional matters and you can use your natural charm to win through almost any situation. People from the past may well be appearing in your life again now.

3 WEDNESDAY
Moon Age Day 21   Moon Sign Cancer

Family relationships could take on a greater importance under present planetary trends, and especially so bearing in mind that the Moon is in your solar fourth house. You can best use these trends by spending some time listening to what your nearest and dearest have to say and leaving more practical matters alone if you can.

4 THURSDAY
Moon Age Day 22   Moon Sign Cancer

Trends encourage a happy-go-lucky frame of mind, and you might be thinking seriously about travel. All at once the real practicalities of life seem to have less importance and you can be fully committed to enjoying yourself. You can afford to let others enjoy this interlude with you.

50

5 FRIDAY
Moon Age Day 23   Moon Sign Leo

Today offers you scope to make those around you as happy as proves to be possible. Your greatest enjoyment could be watching other people enjoy themselves and so everyone wins in the end. In a social sense it is possible for you to begin the weekend one day early and you have what it takes to turn heads romantically.

6 SATURDAY
Moon Age Day 24   Moon Sign Leo

Another lively and enjoyable period is possible, now that the Sun occupies your solar seventh house. The emphasis today is on solid and useful communication. Don't ignore what could turn out to be good advice, even if you think you know better. You might decide to arrange some sort of family outing for tomorrow.

7 SUNDAY
Moon Age Day 25   Moon Sign Leo

Present trends encourage a great need to feel useful, and you may well be pitching around to see to whom you can offer your invaluable services. You think a good deal of yourself at present and there's nothing wrong with that just as long as you come up with the goods when it matters the most.

8 MONDAY
Moon Age Day 26   Moon Sign Virgo

Emotions might now be running high, especially at home. It could be that certain family members have an idea about how they want to behave, whilst you have a very different notion of what's right. Better to discuss things than to lay down the law. Diplomacy isn't always your middle name, but it should be now.

9 TUESDAY
Moon Age Day 27   Moon Sign Virgo

Everything looks as though it will conspire to offer you a potentially positive period as far as work is concerned. Not only is the planet Venus particularly on your side at the moment but the Moon joins in and offers support too. Now you can afford to say what you think and persuade others to give you a really good hearing.

10 WEDNESDAY *Moon Age Day 28 Moon Sign Libra*

It's true that everyday life might have its drawbacks right now, but you can keep yourself on a roll as far as practical issues are concerned. On those occasions when you know you are out of your depth it might be sensible to enlist a little support, even if that means having to go cap in hand to someone.

11 THURSDAY *Moon Age Day 0 Moon Sign Libra*

If your influence over life generally is not as good as you might wish, for that you can thank the lunar low, which stays around both today and tomorrow. The best way forward is slowly, and you can achieve a great deal more at the moment by planning than you can by trying to make concrete progress.

12 FRIDAY ☿ *Moon Age Day 1 Moon Sign Libra*

You are now able to achieve a great deal more in the intimacy stakes, particularly if you are somewhat restricted in other areas of your life. Turning your attention towards love at this time offers a number of benefits. Not least among these is the fact that you can appreciate the warmth that is around you all the time.

13 SATURDAY ☿ *Moon Age Day 2 Moon Sign Scorpio*

It might be appropriate to make certain changes to your life around this time. For example you may decide this is a good time to begin renovations to your home, or it could be that you want to change your car or even buy some new clothes. Really important issues are best left on the shelf until early next week.

14 SUNDAY ☿ *Moon Age Day 3 Moon Sign Scorpio*

You might well be able to attract new friends today, especially if you allow yourself to be persuaded to take part in pastimes that you haven't looked at before. There are always new areas of your nature to explore and you seem to have what it takes today to get on well with a whole host of different people.

YOUR DAILY GUIDE TO OCTOBER 2007

15 MONDAY ☿ *Moon Age Day 4* *Moon Sign Sagittarius*

You benefit from mental stimulation and could do worse that to pit your wits against someone you consider to be a worthy adversary. Aries tendencies are really on display if you are competitive and filled with a desire to be the best. The only disappointment comes when you realise that this is not always the case.

16 TUESDAY ☿ *Moon Age Day 5* *Moon Sign Sagittarius*

Rowdy arguments simply will not solve problems at the present time and you would be much better off discussing matters in a sensible way or else withdrawing from situations of confrontation altogether. If you can stay peaceful with yourself and the world at large, you should get a great deal more done.

17 WEDNESDAY ☿ *Moon Age Day 6* *Moon Sign Sagittarius*

There are trends about presently that empower you to take actions and to improve certain conditions, especially in your workplace. If routines prove to be something of a bore, it is important to ring the changes as much as possible in order to get the very most out of your life during this interlude.

18 THURSDAY ☿ *Moon Age Day 7* *Moon Sign Capricorn*

You may now be sensitive to the moods of others and show a greater tendency than usual to adapt to prevailing circumstances. Even if you can't get everything you want today, if you approach those around you in the proper way you can get very close. Why not look at the present circumstances of a friend and offer some practical help?

19 FRIDAY ☿ *Moon Age Day 8* *Moon Sign Capricorn*

Today's insights are steady, enabling you to be a good deal more thoughtful than has been the case across recent days. This is a particularly good time for solving any sort of problem, and it doesn't matter whether this occurs at a practical level or if you are simply spending time with a crossword puzzle.

20 SATURDAY ☿ *Moon Age Day 9   Moon Sign Aquarius*

Trends suggest you have a strong need for friendship, and may well decide to turn to those you have known for some time in order to reassure yourself that they are still as committed to you as they were. As far as this weekend is concerned you may well prefer to have people around you most of the time and should enjoy their presence.

21 SUNDAY ☿ *Moon Age Day 10   Moon Sign Aquarius*

Domestic issues are highlighted, and may take up a great deal of your time today, so you mightn't be able to spend much time thinking about work or purely practical issues. Turn to people you haven't had much to do with of late and learn what they have been doing recently. There could be a revelation in store.

22 MONDAY ☿ *Moon Age Day 11   Moon Sign Pisces*

A greater desire than usual for solitude is a possibility, and for this you can thank the position of the Moon, which now occupies your solar twelfth house. By being quiet and contemplative you can learn a great deal more about yourself than would be the case if you bluster about aimlessly.

23 TUESDAY ☿ *Moon Age Day 12   Moon Sign Pisces*

You can move practical matters along quite nicely, even if your nature still doesn't have the edge that it will in a day or two. Acting on impulse is not to be recommended for the moment and you should achieve far more if you let those around you know in advance how you intend to act. There is a strong need for continuity at present.

24 WEDNESDAY ☿ *Moon Age Day 13   Moon Sign Pisces*

Getting down to the root of personal issues or practical problems is recommended for today. Your intuition is potentially strong and you should not turn away from any deeply held conviction, even on those occasions when you don't understand where the feelings are coming from. Slow and steady wins the race today.

25 THURSDAY ☿ *Moon Age Day 14 Moon Sign Aries*

The lunar high arrives and offers all manner of new incentives, together with the most positive attitude you have probably experienced during the whole of this month. Now is the time to decide what you want in a practical or professional sense and go for it. Controlling a number of different issues at the same time should be easy.

26 FRIDAY ☿ *Moon Age Day 15 Moon Sign Aries*

If you need assistance you have what it takes to find it at the moment. You can get things to go your way, and can make this one of the best days of October right now. Make the most of the attitude of those with whom you have to deal in a moment-by-moment sense, as it offers you important new incentives.

27 SATURDAY ☿ *Moon Age Day 16 Moon Sign Taurus*

A favourable time is on offer, during which you can strengthen your personal affairs, and today also marks a time when you can look seriously at expenditure and money generally. Although there might be a few dull issues to deal with, in the main you can take this opportunity to ring the changes.

28 SUNDAY ☿ *Moon Age Day 17 Moon Sign Taurus*

There are signs that you might find yourself somewhat at odds with those you have to rely on the most in a momentary sense, and this may be particularly true in your home life. Avoid getting on the wrong side of a particular individual who is in a position to do you some good in the days and weeks ahead. Diplomacy is called for.

29 MONDAY ☿ *Moon Age Day 18 Moon Sign Gemini*

Even if ordinary matters predominate right now, you still have scope to do something more exciting and need to explore a few possibilities. Today offers opportunities to broaden the scope of your interests, and you might also find that romance has a greater part to play in your life than has been the case recently.

30 TUESDAY ☿ *Moon Age Day 19 Moon Sign Gemini*

Advising other people is to the fore today and a few of them will surprise you because they normally seem to give you a wide berth. Don't be too quick to make up your mind about anything. It would be sensible to wait and see in a few specific cases, and even to stop some of your projects altogether.

31 WEDNESDAY ☿ *Moon Age Day 20 Moon Sign Cancer*

Trends suggest that family and personal matters will predominate today, and as the month draws to a close you may also be thinking carefully about those last jobs you want to do around the house before winter begins to settle in. Below the surface there may also be a burning desire to do something quite different and maybe a little exciting.

November

2007

1 THURSDAY ☿ *Moon Age Day 21   Moon Sign Cancer*

This is a good day for getting together with your partner, family members and close friends. Even if you sense there is plenty to get done in a practical sense, perhaps this really doesn't matter for now. You can afford simply to be yourself and enjoy good company whilst it is on offer. Some real personalities could be entering your life.

2 FRIDAY ☿ *Moon Age Day 22   Moon Sign Leo*

You can subject certain aspects of your life to a little regeneration at this time and should be quite willing to look at all issues in a very new light. Standard responses probably don't work very well at work, and you need to think of ways to show a greater degree of originality if you can.

3 SATURDAY *Moon Age Day 23   Moon Sign Leo*

Mercury is now in your solar seventh house, a position from where it stimulates your need for communication and simple companionship. You may be drawn to friends and especially those who have played a part in your life for some years. Be willing to modify your opinions whenever it proves to be advantageous.

4 SUNDAY *Moon Age Day 24   Moon Sign Virgo*

You can now explore new ways of approaching the world, and have what it takes to come up with revolutionary new ideas that others find difficult to understand. Explaining yourself is what today is all about because you have it within you to bring almost anyone round to your way of thinking if you plan your strategy first.

5 MONDAY
Moon Age Day 25   Moon Sign Virgo

You have a chance to get rid of any outworn elements of your life around this time. The present position of the Sun in your solar chart brings a period during which you should be happy to dump anything that is no longer of any use to you. Why not enlist family members to help in this important process?

6 TUESDAY
Moon Age Day 26   Moon Sign Libra

Don't make life any more difficult for yourself than you have to. The lunar low comes along at this time and could sap some of your strength and determination. It might be better to leave certain tasks on hold for a day or two than to risk getting things wrong and having to start all over again later.

7 WEDNESDAY
Moon Age Day 27   Moon Sign Libra

A time to stick to tried and tested methods for getting what you want and avoid new fads and fancies. It's the reliable old you that works best at the moment and you should avoid listening to anyone who claims to have discovered every shortcut in the book. You can rely on the friends who have been around you for some time.

8 THURSDAY
Moon Age Day 28   Moon Sign Libra

Getting ahead should still definitely not be an issue in your mind. By tomorrow things look different and you will once again be able to start the process of getting rid of surplus baggage. For the moment you are not seeing things clearly enough to make the right decisions. Relying on the support of family members would be no bad thing.

9 FRIDAY
Moon Age Day 0   Moon Sign Scorpio

The romantic side of life now comes to the fore, and having left the lunar low behind you, the sky looks blue again, no matter what the weather is doing outside. By being active and enterprising you can show a really positive face to the world and particularly to the person who is most important to you.

10 SATURDAY   *Moon Age Day 1   Moon Sign Scorpio*

You have scope to influence family members under present trends, and could be spending more time thinking about domestic issues than professional ones. Friends may also be demanding your attention, something that is unlikely to bother you at all whilst Mars occupies your solar fourth house.

11 SUNDAY   *Moon Age Day 2   Moon Sign Sagittarius*

A real sense of regeneration remains a fundamental component of your life and thinking at this time. This is a phase that is set to continue for at least another week, and marks an important period for coming to terms with the fact that not everything can stay the way it was. A clean sweep is definitely possible.

12 MONDAY   *Moon Age Day 3   Moon Sign Sagittarius*

Extended travel might seem particularly attractive around now and some Aries subjects will be thinking about journeys that are thousands of miles in length. Beware of being too quick to judge the motivations of colleagues or friends because even if it doesn't look that way, they may actually have your interests at heart.

13 TUESDAY   *Moon Age Day 4   Moon Sign Sagittarius*

This has potential to be a wonderful day and one where personal attachments are specifically highlighted. You are able to find exactly the right words to show your nearest and dearest just how important they are to you, and can also show tremendous support to those friends who occupy centre stage in your thinking.

14 WEDNESDAY   *Moon Age Day 5   Moon Sign Capricorn*

Trends right now assist you to attune yourself to whatever stimulates others, and so getting on side with them shouldn't be difficult. Your best form of progress now comes through a willingness to share and to be part of something that is definitely bigger than you are. Your charitable qualities are also well accented at present.

15 THURSDAY   *Moon Age Day 6   Moon Sign Capricorn*

Professional matters can be given a very pleasant and possibly unexpected boost under present trends. There is now a greater tendency for you to act on impulse and the planetary line-up shows that you can get away with doing so. You can persuade people to respond to your spontaneity and willingly follow your lead.

16 FRIDAY   *Moon Age Day 7   Moon Sign Aquarius*

The best gains today can be made by being exactly what you are – an Aries subject. Even if not everyone falls in line with either your thinking or your actions, that doesn't really matter. Those who can are going to be at your shoulder but there may always be one or two people who fall by the wayside.

17 SATURDAY   *Moon Age Day 8   Moon Sign Aquarius*

Venus is now in your solar seventh house, a position from where it has a great bearing on all types of relationships. From the most casual nodding acknowledgement to the love of your life, your ability to get on with those around you is second to none. Much of the progress possible now is related to your present friendliness.

18 SUNDAY   *Moon Age Day 9   Moon Sign Aquarius*

Finances could tend to fluctuate somewhat around now and you need to be just a little more careful in the way you handle money. It could be sensible to ask the advice of someone older or wiser, whilst at the same time giving an eye to the longer-term future and ways you can lay up cash now for decades ahead.

19 MONDAY   *Moon Age Day 10   Moon Sign Pisces*

Social pursuits have potential to capture your imagination and you should be more than willing to join in with whatever is going on in your immediate circle. There are ways in which you can mix business with pleasure, whilst at the same time making profit out of the most unpromising situations. Ingenuity is the key to success at present.

20 TUESDAY   *Moon Age Day 11   Moon Sign Pisces*

By tomorrow there is little to stand in your way, but for the first part of today at least you are likely to be showing a much quieter face to the world at large. Thoughtful and even contemplative, you may decide that a particular course of action needs modifying and could spend several hours working things out.

21 WEDNESDAY   *Moon Age Day 12   Moon Sign Aries*

The Moon is back in your zodiac sign of Aries and now comes the time for taking those half-exploited ideas and making them work the way you would wish. Almost anything is possible now and something that looked absolutely impossible once upon a time can seem commonplace because of your own effort.

22 THURSDAY   *Moon Age Day 13   Moon Sign Aries*

The positive trends continue and extend to the fact that you are able to see ahead positively for the benefit of loved ones as well as for yourself. Acting on impulse is likely to be second nature, and you can show a degree of vivacity that lifts you in the eyes of almost everyone you meet. This is a red-letter day for some Aries people.

23 FRIDAY   *Moon Age Day 14   Moon Sign Taurus*

Getting on side with those around you could be a piece of cake right now. Even people you have always thought of as being awkward in the past can now be brought under your influence, and you have exactly what it takes to make situations work out the way you want them to.

24 SATURDAY   *Moon Age Day 15   Moon Sign Taurus*

Tensions could arise at home, and these need to be dealt with very carefully if you are to avoid unnecessary and probably slightly destructive rows. Getting your loved ones to see sense may not always be easy, but you have also to be aware that what is self-evident to you might not seem that way to others.

25 SUNDAY · Moon Age Day 16 · Moon Sign Gemini

The present position of Venus enhances your naturally romantic frame of mind and assists you to get to grips with personal attachments. The time is right to keep an open mind about necessary changes within your domestic sphere and to look ahead just a little to the festive season, which is only a month away.

26 MONDAY · Moon Age Day 17 · Moon Sign Gemini

You benefit now from a more open approach and it is vital that you explain yourself to almost everyone. You have what it takes to persuade others to show a great deal of interest in your ideas around this time and to move mountains, if only you employ the more sensible side of your nature. Aries should be well on top under present trends.

27 TUESDAY · Moon Age Day 18 · Moon Sign Cancer

There are some unexpected gains for the taking around now, and some of these will be almost totally unexpected. Showing a great sensitivity to the feelings of others, you can also be active and enterprising for some days to come. Your nature is extremely well balanced at this juncture.

28 WEDNESDAY · Moon Age Day 19 · Moon Sign Cancer

Trends suggest that pressure could be slightly stepped up at home, and it is important not to rise to the bait of people who are being deliberately provocative. Instead of firing from the hip, be willing to look at matters carefully and to reserve your judgement under most circumstances. You can get what you want, but it might take a little while.

29 THURSDAY · Moon Age Day 20 · Moon Sign Leo

The impact of your personality cannot be underestimated, and you can definitely have more of an impression on people than you might immediately realise. Impressing people who really count should be easier, and there is a chance that you can achieve a real advancement soon.

30 FRIDAY
Moon Age Day 21   Moon Sign Leo

You can take advantage of a definite peak any time now. There are a number of strong planetary influences working well on your behalf and there are gains to be made in a host of different directions. If there is any problem at the moment it revolves around knowing what to tackle next.

♈

December

2007

1 SATURDAY   *Moon Age Day 22   Moon Sign Virgo*

It is possible that at home your emotional needs may conflict with
the practical aspects of getting things done. What is necessary today
won't be what you want, and a slight conflict could start to develop
as a result. Your best approach is to keep ahead of necessary tasks
and prepare yourself today for something that is important early
next week.

2 SUNDAY   *Moon Age Day 23   Moon Sign Virgo*

This could be a fairly low-key sort of day, which might seem hard
after such a bevy of positive days. All the same there are gains to be
made, even if these are only really centred upon your ability to get
on the same wavelength as family members and in particular your
life partner.

3 MONDAY   *Moon Age Day 24   Moon Sign Virgo*

Although today might be rather quieter than you expected, it does
have its good points. For one thing you can be very attentive to the
natures and needs of those around you. Sorting out your own
problems today shouldn't really be an issue, but you will be in a
position to offer some timely assistance where it's needed the most.

4 TUESDAY   *Moon Age Day 25   Moon Sign Libra*

A few compromises might have to be made whilst the lunar low is
about and you may also have to work that much harder to get what
you want out of today. There are some very useful planetary
positions in your solar chart, so it's possible that the position of the
Moon will have less of a bearing on you generally than might
usually be the case.

5 WEDNESDAY   *Moon Age Day 26   Moon Sign Libra*

A day to keep your expectations reasonably low and not to be too anxious to get ahead. You would be better off planning rather than doing anything specific at this time, and allowing those around you to take some of the strain. There ought to be time to think and to recharge batteries that may be flagging a little.

6 THURSDAY   *Moon Age Day 27   Moon Sign Scorpio*

Why not get down to basics today and put into action some of the plans you thought about across the last couple of days? You have more energy available now, and a greater sense of determination to get things the way you want them. This would be especially true in the case of your profession.

7 FRIDAY   *Moon Age Day 28   Moon Sign Scorpio*

The monetary side of life is well accented at the moment, and it's possible that you have an idea at the back of your head that will see you somehow better off in the days ahead. Ingenuity is second nature to Aries, and especially so under prevailing planetary trends. Now is the time to be bold and determined.

8 SATURDAY   *Moon Age Day 29   Moon Sign Scorpio*

This is not a good time to be putting pressure on people at home. You can afford to let things ride for a while and give people the time and space they need to make up their own minds. There are gains to be made from simply watching and waiting, and this applies as much to the practical side of life as to anything else.

9 SUNDAY   *Moon Age Day 0   Moon Sign Sagittarius*

Everything that is going on around you can bring its own rewards at this time. Boundless energy is available all of a sudden but you may decide to expend this on family members or friends on a Sunday. Plans for Christmas might be in full swing and there is something warm about the feelings engendered.

10 MONDAY   *Moon Age Day 1   Moon Sign Sagittarius*

You tend to be quite chatty now, and can get a good deal of information simply by being yourself. Although you might decide to defer one or two of your schemes, your mind is probably working overtime and it's fair to suggest that you show a greater ingenuity around this time than has been the case for quite a while.

11 TUESDAY   *Moon Age Day 2   Moon Sign Capricorn*

You can be right on the ball when it comes to initiating new schemes, and there isn't much doubt about your capabilities. Bear in mind that others may be watching you closely, and this ought to be one of the best times of the month to get yourself noticed. There are some fairly unexpected gains becoming possible under present planetary trends.

12 WEDNESDAY   *Moon Age Day 3   Moon Sign Capricorn*

You could end up allowing powerful emotions to get in the way of your practical common sense, not a state of affairs that is very useful right now. You would be wise to try to stay cool, calm and collected at all times, and if you can't manage to do so, you could spend some time on your own so that others won't see your reactions.

13 THURSDAY   *Moon Age Day 4   Moon Sign Capricorn*

The Moon is in your solar eleventh house, a position from where it assists you to bring out the best in yourself. Conforming to the expectations of others may not be easy, but you have sufficient cheek to get away with just about anything now. Your reaction time under all circumstances should be even faster than usual.

14 FRIDAY   *Moon Age Day 5   Moon Sign Aquarius*

You can afford to extend yourself into unknown areas and be willing to tackle jobs that you might have shied away from in the past. People you don't see too often could be coming into your life again and are likely to offer you a new way of looking at an old situation. Concentration is good, and your powers of perception highlighted.

15 SATURDAY   *Moon Age Day 6   Moon Sign Aquarius*

There are gains to be made if you can avoid the usual tedious routines and try to get as many new influences into your life as proves to be possible. It might be slightly difficult to fall in line with the notions of people you think are idiots, but you can feather your own nest by showing a willingness to follow their lead.

16 SUNDAY   *Moon Age Day 7   Moon Sign Pisces*

This is a potentially favourable time for financial matters and especially for looking again at any issues from the past that have been shelved for some time. Ingenuity is a hallmark of your nature at the moment and you have what it takes to put in that extra bit of thought that can make all the difference in the end.

17 MONDAY   *Moon Age Day 8   Moon Sign Pisces*

The Moon is now in your solar twelfth house and this makes for an excellent day to be working on your own. It isn't that you have any difficulty getting on with others. On the contrary, your popularity could be going off the scale at the moment. It's simply that you may be more efficient when tackling things in your own way.

18 TUESDAY   *Moon Age Day 9   Moon Sign Aries*

The lunar high assists you to tackle several different tasks at the same time. You have what it takes to get ahead in almost any sphere of your life and demonstrate just how capable you are when it matters the most. If thoughts of Christmas are on your mind, why not sort out a few practical necessities today?

19 WEDNESDAY   *Moon Age Day 10   Moon Sign Aries*

You should still be in good form and able to tackle things that would have intimidated even you earlier in the month. With everything to play for and plenty of energy at your command, this is the time to put in that essential push ahead of the festive season. There should also be hours available in which to simply enjoy yourself.

20 THURSDAY   *Moon Age Day 11   Moon Sign Taurus*

Your practical energies are best directed towards work, and you should still be feeling on top form. Even if you have difficulty getting on side with one or two people, when it matters the most you can adapt your own nature to suit theirs. Trends encourage you to be especially compassionate at the moment.

21 FRIDAY   *Moon Age Day 12   Moon Sign Taurus*

You need to think fairly seriously about your own career direction at present, though this may not be easy at a time of year when there are many distractions pressing in on you. Prepare yourself for an enforced lay-off during the Christmas period, and make sure that you have your plans well laid in advance.

22 SATURDAY   *Moon Age Day 13   Moon Sign Gemini*

Relationships are highlighted, and this area of life is coming good at just the right time. You should be present to help with arrangements and can even be experiencing distinct periods of nostalgia – something that doesn't happen very much to Aries people. Pleasing others seems to be very significant at present.

23 SUNDAY   *Moon Age Day 14   Moon Sign Gemini*

Trends suggest you will enjoy being on the move and won't be at all pleased if you find yourself being restricted in any way. Don't be too worried if something you see as important has to take second place to pleasing family members. There is always another day, and you don't want to appear too distracted to join in socially.

24 MONDAY   *Moon Age Day 15   Moon Sign Cancer*

The Moon is now in your solar fourth house and that puts you firmly in the area of home and family as far as your thinking is concerned. This might encourage you to be quieter and more contemplative than has been the case in the recent past and to show the greatest consideration possible to the needs of others.

25 TUESDAY   *Moon Age Day 16   Moon Sign Cancer*

Although Christmas Day could prove to be extremely happy, it also has its demands. Your own ruling planet Mars is conjunct with the Moon in your solar fourth house and so a good deal of patience will be necessary. Add to this a few minor frustrations and it's clear that you have your work cut out in order to smile all day.

26 WEDNESDAY   *Moon Age Day 17   Moon Sign Leo*

A marvellous sense of emotional closeness becomes possible, and with less pressure on you, this might be the most enjoyable of the two main holidays of Christmas. You could feel drawn towards intimate moments and show a warmth and sensitivity for which your zodiac sign of Aries is not generally famous.

27 THURSDAY   *Moon Age Day 18   Moon Sign Leo*

A lively and extroverted influence is brought about by the changing position of the Moon. Active and enterprising, you need to be out of the house and finding ways to use up some of the surplus energy that surges through you at the moment. Even if you still show significant sensitivity, it could be overpowered by a need to act.

28 FRIDAY   *Moon Age Day 19   Moon Sign Leo*

You can make this quite a progressive time in a general sense, which is only slightly spoiled if there are demands being made of you that are difficult to deal with. There is something of a split between your sense of loyalty to your family and your simple, raw need to get on with life at a practical level.

29 SATURDAY   *Moon Age Day 20   Moon Sign Virgo*

The domestic sphere might be upset by arguments that are not only needless but actually totally ridiculous. The best way forward for you is to refuse to be drawn into such situations. Playing the honest broker is fine, but not if this means you have to take sides in such a way that you become directly involved.

30 SUNDAY
Moon Age Day 21   Moon Sign Virgo

It is obvious that you have what it takes to keep up a very high profile today and to attract plenty of attention. With the festivities probably still going on all around you, it seems as though you are tired of enjoying yourself and want to get on with some of the practical plans that have been on your mind for a while.

31 MONDAY
Moon Age Day 22   Moon Sign Libra

It might not be easy to be happy-go-lucky at a time when the Moon occupies your opposite zodiac sign. All the same you should be able to put a smile on your face and to enjoy the passing of the old year. Don't be surprised if you prefer the company of people you know very well because you may shun strangers slightly.

ARIES:
2008 DIARY PAGES

ARIES:
2008 IN BRIEF

The accent is definitely on success for Aries this year, even if there are a few slight distractions on the way. Starting very positively, January and February bring a great start to the year and offer new incentives at work. Despite the winter you are progressive, anxious to travel and happy to do whatever is necessary to get ahead. People from the past emerge into your life again and bring with them a few memories that are difficult to avoid.

March and April bring the spring and add a little extra incentive to your efforts, particularly at home. This is a time for making changes to your home surroundings and for getting family matters sorted out. Don't be slow when it comes to meeting new incentives at work head-on. April can be especially rewarding in a financial sense and may also see you sweeping someone off their feet.

With the later spring May and June see things slowing down just a little but the incentive to get ahead is still present. You might have to rely more on the good offices of others at this time but you will still be anxious to stamp your own authority on most situations. Love comes knocking for some at this time and romance grows along with the first rich blossoms of the year. Make the most of new friendships and also the chance of encountering someone who is probably quite famous. Standard responses to old problems won't work at this time.

By July you will be enjoying what the summer has to offer and it is at this time that your absolute desire to spread your wings and fly becomes most obvious. Both long and short journeys will be possible, both for business and for pleasure. Make this a time to open a new dialogue with people who might have been difficult to deal with in the past and also plan well financially. August continues the favourable trends but could find you facing slight personal frustrations.

September and October might be somewhat quieter, though this is not to suggest your life is standing still at this time. On the contrary you are making progress, but it is simply that you are taking situations one at a time and will be less likely to gamble. Personalities surround you on all sides and much of your attention during October is given to family members and domestic situations.

The final two months of the year, November and December, see you once again out there at the front and in the position you love the most. Some patience will be necessary with others, particularly in November, but there are personal gains to be had and a rich and happy period in the weeks running up towards Christmas. The festive period itself could be characterised by surprise events and exciting meetings.

January
2008

1 TUESDAY
Moon Age Day 23   Moon Sign Libra

What you need most of all at the moment is a sense of freedom from obligations, so the end of the Christmas holidays probably can't come too soon as far as you are concerned. It's also time to get your thinking cap on because there are plans to be laid that could enable you to get on very much better at work or in social situations.

2 WEDNESDAY
Moon Age Day 24   Moon Sign Libra

If there are sacrifices to be made at the moment, especially on behalf of your family, you would do well not to play on the fact that you are putting yourself out. The more generous of spirit you are, the greater can be the accolades that you can attract from the direction of those around you. Be prepared to strengthen your finances.

3 THURSDAY
Moon Age Day 25   Moon Sign Scorpio

If you use your drive and determination you can get the things that you say today to go straight to the heart of any matter. The directness of Aries can be put on display and you shouldn't have any trouble at all making the sort of impression for which your zodiac sign is justifiably famous. Don't over-commit yourself.

4 FRIDAY
Moon Age Day 26   Moon Sign Scorpio

Your penchant for unusual experiences is potentially on display at the moment and you might decide to take a chance or two if that means seeing new sights and meeting some fairly unusual sorts of people. Even if family members are quite demanding at present, you should take this in your stride pretty well.

5 SATURDAY · Moon Age Day 27 · Moon Sign Sagittarius

If you happen to work at the weekend, today could be the best day of the week for getting on well professionally. If, on the other hand, your time is your own, you have scope to think up new ways of getting on well, especially with anyone who has given you a problem in the recent past.

6 SUNDAY · Moon Age Day 28 · Moon Sign Sagittarius

You thrive on communications of all kinds and should have little or no trouble getting on well with just about everyone on this Sunday. Your ability to get out and about might be somewhat hampered by the winter weather, but it is worth putting on a good, thick coat and getting some fresh air, no matter what the conditions may be.

7 MONDAY · Moon Age Day 29 · Moon Sign Sagittarius

At this time you have what it takes to be a natural leader, and shouldn't have much trouble getting others to follow your lead. Avoid arguing for your limitations but at the same time try to find that humble quality in your nature that others respect. It's a fine line because you also need to show how confident you can truly be.

8 TUESDAY · Moon Age Day 0 · Moon Sign Capricorn

There is now good scope for professional advancement and you could do worse than asking for a raise or arguing for more responsibility whilst the astrological picture looks so good. Once again you need to be slightly careful and should avoid being too pushy. With a little tact and diplomacy you can probably get anything you want.

9 WEDNESDAY · Moon Age Day 1 · Moon Sign Capricorn

Influences surrounding friendships and group matters are well accented in your mind around this time. Family commitments might seem to hold you back a little, but in the main you can get on well with almost everyone. Of course there are bound to be exceptions, but that's the nature of life and you can take it in your stride.

10 THURSDAY   *Moon Age Day 2*   *Moon Sign Aquarius*

Trends encourage plenty of variety and you may not take kindly to being held back by circumstances that are beyond your own control. If you show patience and take the rough with the smooth you can gain great support from those around you. Try to ring the changes socially and put yourself in positions that assure you of new friends.

11 FRIDAY   *Moon Age Day 3*   *Moon Sign Aquarius*

Even if you are willing to work very hard to gain your objectives, the problem is that the same may not be true of people with whom you have to co-operate. There may be times now when your best option is simply to do your own thing, even if that means waiting around later for other slower types to catch up with you.

12 SATURDAY   *Moon Age Day 4*   *Moon Sign Pisces*

It's worth listening carefully to what your instincts are telling you because this is a time during which they are unlikely to let you down. Practical common sense is not quite so good as gut reactions for the moment, and though you are hardly likely to lose touch with reality, you could find certain situations working out rather strangely.

13 SUNDAY   *Moon Age Day 5*   *Moon Sign Pisces*

Your critical qualities are potentially showing out well today and you needn't take anything at face value. This may annoy others somewhat, particularly if there are disagreements about the way things should be done. Once again it's important to follow your instincts, which are unlikely to be wrong.

14 MONDAY   *Moon Age Day 6*   *Moon Sign Pisces*

Later today the Moon returns to your own zodiac sign today bringing that part of the month that is known as the lunar high. For the next couple of days you can use this influence to make progress, and you need to be as definite and positive as proves to be the case. Routines would probably bore you now.

15 TUESDAY   *Moon Age Day 7   Moon Sign Aries*

A day to put your best foot forward and be willing to undertake anything that seems to be even remotely possible. Every one of your reactions has potential to be good, and if you can't succeed at present it is probably because you are not putting in sufficient effort. People from the past who emerge again now might well bring some surprises.

16 WEDNESDAY   *Moon Age Day 8   Moon Sign Aries*

Your best approach is to keep moving forward and show the world at large what you are made of. Even if someone is trying to throw a spanner in the works, probably at work, you got out of bed very early today and shouldn't allow any of your plans to be diverted, particularly if you know that what you have in mind is going to work out well for you.

17 THURSDAY   *Moon Age Day 9   Moon Sign Taurus*

Hectic communications of one sort or another seem to be the way forward, and in any case there may be little you can do about the frenetic quality of your life. Someone you don't know very well might become ever more important to you, and it is possible that some Aries subjects may decide to embark on a new romance soon.

18 FRIDAY   *Moon Age Day 10   Moon Sign Taurus*

An ideal time to assert your views and opinions because to do so enhances your nature and makes you important to those around you. It's probably the end of the working week as far as you are concerned and it looks as though you can start the weekend early. If routines can be a bore, you would be best off leaving them alone.

19 SATURDAY   *Moon Age Day 11   Moon Sign Gemini*

You can now attract help and support from some rather unusual directions, and you would be rather foolish to turn away what is so freely offered. Don't be afraid to stick out your neck if your opinions are being sought by others. The fact is that they know you to be both sensible and clear thinking, and will trust you.

20 SUNDAY
Moon Age Day 12   Moon Sign Gemini

Domestic and family life should be positive areas for you, and where there have been difficulties or disagreements in the past, you can now pour oil on troubled water. Aries is not the most diplomatic of the zodiac signs as a rule, but at the moment you have it within your power to sort out just about any kind of past difficulty.

21 MONDAY
Moon Age Day 13   Moon Sign Cancer

Your way of dealing with personal difficulties remains both sensible and wise. If not everyone is behaving as well as they might, it will be up to you to make some real allowances, which allow those around you an escape route from their own foolishness. Attitude is particularly important when it comes to your working life.

22 TUESDAY
Moon Age Day 14   Moon Sign Cancer

Today's trends help you to show yourself to be a born entertainer, and you shouldn't have any trouble enlivening the most mundane of gatherings. You have what it takes at present to hold any audience in the palm of your hand. Keep your sense of humour.

23 WEDNESDAY
Moon Age Day 15   Moon Sign Leo

Positive in your dealings with both friends and colleagues, now is the time to push for something you really want. This doesn't mean bulldozing others so that they accept your point of view, but rather showing how genuinely persuasive you are capable of being. Love shines out as being extremely important to you at present.

24 THURSDAY
Moon Age Day 16   Moon Sign Leo

In professional matters you can really be on the ball, which is why others may be seeking your point of view and following your lead at the moment. You can persuade everyone you meet to be positive in their attitude and all it takes from you is to maintain your diplomatic frame of mind and to approach people in the right way.

25 FRIDAY   *Moon Age Day 17   Moon Sign Virgo*

Even if you still have plenty of energy when it comes to work, in a social sense you may be growing slightly quieter. You might decide to settle for an evening during which you could put up your feet and watch the television, but there is a strong possibility that life itself will have different ideas. Try to go with the flow.

26 SATURDAY   *Moon Age Day 18   Moon Sign Virgo*

A time to put yourself in the social limelight and to make sure you are everyone's cup of tea. Of course you can't be universally popular, and it's the essence of your nature that there will be competitors about too. Why not sort out the wheat from the chaff and concentrate on those individuals who offer the most?

27 SUNDAY   *Moon Age Day 19   Moon Sign Libra*

This may not be the best time of the month for you. The Moon now occupies your opposite zodiac sign of Libra, bringing that time known as the lunar low. For the moment it would be best to rest and to recharge your batteries, whilst you allow others to take some of the strain and to make the most of the really important decisions.

28 MONDAY   *Moon Age Day 20   Moon Sign Libra*

If things are still fairly quiet in your life, this can bring its own frustrations, especially since it is the essence of your basic nature to be in charge of everything. You might decide to give way to the opinions of people you trust because it is now exhausting and pointless to argue about matters that you are not exactly sure about anyway.

29 TUESDAY   ☿   *Moon Age Day 21   Moon Sign Libra*

You have scope to be intuitive and to show others that you are thinking deeply about life. By just after the middle of the day the Moon moves on and offers a stronger sense of purpose for you. With the lunar low out of the way you have what it takes to shoot forward like a bullet out of a gun, but might need to be careful not to try and do too much.

30 WEDNESDAY ☿ *Moon Age Day 22 Moon Sign Scorpio*

A much-heightened appreciation of others helps you to do all you can to show them how important they are to you. Your natural generosity really begins to shine out and there are gains to be made in a number of different directions simply by bearing in mind the needs and wants of your loved ones.

31 THURSDAY ☿ *Moon Age Day 23 Moon Sign Scorpio*

'The more, the merrier' seems to be the best adage for you today, both in terms of the number of people who come into your life and with regard to the plethora of things you decide to take on. Don't get tied down by routines, and where possible cut through the red tape of any situations that seem over-complicated or filled with provisos.

February
2008

1 FRIDAY
☿ *Moon Age Day 24*   *Moon Sign Sagittarius*

It's the first day of February and although the world is wrapped in the midst of winter, as far as you are concerned you do need to ring the changes as much as possible and to get out into the good fresh air. Allowing yourself to be kept in some sort of cage is definitely out. Freedom is always important to Aries, but especially so at the moment.

2 SATURDAY
☿ *Moon Age Day 25*   *Moon Sign Sagittarius*

The weekend should offer a chance to achieve bright and happy moments, and especially so if you look around you and show yourself to be willing to change with altering circumstances. Give yourself a pat on the back with regard to some recent success, but this is certainly not a time to be smug. You need to keep on pushing forward.

3 SUNDAY
☿ *Moon Age Day 26*   *Moon Sign Sagittarius*

You would be wise to avoid hasty actions today and move along slowly and steadily towards your objectives. The present position of the Moon suggests that you could come unstuck if you allow yourself to be moved by every little factor that crops up. Mainstream thinking and actions that are well-defined are definitely the way forward.

4 MONDAY
☿ *Moon Age Day 27*   *Moon Sign Capricorn*

You may well be able to attract extra support today for long-term plans, but if you do be sure to give credit where it's due. Almost anyone could be doing you a favour at present, even people you previously thought of as competitors. Maybe you were wrong in your assessment of them, and need to show a friendly face?

5 TUESDAY ☿ *Moon Age Day 28* *Moon Sign Capricorn*

Mars is now in your solar third house and that offers you a chance to show your lightning wit and the ability to come back at others quickly with remarks that should keep everyone laughing. Be careful that you don't offer unintended offence to someone who is of a really sensitive nature. Routines can be boring today, but will be necessary.

6 WEDNESDAY ☿ *Moon Age Day 0* *Moon Sign Aquarius*

This would be an excellent day to be with your friends and to enjoy the cut and thrust of a particularly interesting social life. OK, so the weather may still be awful and you might not be getting out into the fresh air too much, but at least you can seek out people who think you are great and you can also make practical progress.

7 THURSDAY ☿ *Moon Age Day 1* *Moon Sign Aquarius*

Today you can show yourself to be very outgoing and demonstrate a willing spirit, as well as generosity in a more practical sense. You tend to be the leader in most situations and this is especially true right now. Confidence shouldn't be lacking and you can push through some plans that have been on hold for a while.

8 FRIDAY ☿ *Moon Age Day 2* *Moon Sign Aquarius*

Trends encourage you to make some important concessions as far as others are concerned and to try to put right something that went wrong quite some time ago. Even if you keep one eye on the past, you shouldn't forget to put in the sort of effort right now that will pay great dividends.

9 SATURDAY ☿ *Moon Age Day 3* *Moon Sign Pisces*

With the Moon in your solar twelfth house the very sensitive side of your nature can be put on display. You could be slightly quieter at the moment, but this interlude comes ahead of a great boost to your energy. It could be quite useful to simple think about things for an hour or two – instead of dashing into the fray as you usually do.

10 SUNDAY ☿ *Moon Age Day 4   Moon Sign Pisces*

You still might not be exactly dynamic but that's fine because this is a time during which you can plan, rather than a time for putting those plans into action. By tomorrow everything will change and you can be back to your usual self. Today would be good for catching up with the needs of specific family members.

11 MONDAY ☿ *Moon Age Day 5   Moon Sign Aries*

With the Moon now back in your own zodiac sign you have scope to be full of beans and to make the best of impressions when it counts the most. You can request help from others if you need it, but that won't be often because you know exactly what you want and have a good idea how to get it.

12 TUESDAY ☿ *Moon Age Day 6   Moon Sign Aries*

A day to give your career the right sort of support, some of which comes from less than expected directions. If you are between positions this is the best time of the month in which to look around. Your powers of persuasion have rarely been better and if there is something you particularly want, now is the time to ask for it.

13 WEDNESDAY ☿ *Moon Age Day 7   Moon Sign Taurus*

You may well benefit from working with others on projects that will work out to your mutual satisfaction. Some Aries people may be setting up partnerships around now and these are likely to work out best if you think about the details carefully. Beware of putting your name to anything today unless you have read the small print.

14 THURSDAY ☿ *Moon Age Day 8   Moon Sign Taurus*

Venus is now in your solar tenth house and this brings a period of helpful professional influences, together with a chance to use some of your charm. The finer and more creative side of your nature can be put on display and one expression of this will be your determination to have your home surroundings just the way you want.

15 FRIDAY ☿ *Moon Age Day 9   Moon Sign Gemini*

This is a good time for communication and mental interests generally. Now you have scope to debate, to write letters and emails and to send a whole series of interesting text messages. The mechanical side of your mind is also well highlighted and so if you have to take something to pieces, it's worth getting on with it sometime today.

16 SATURDAY ☿ *Moon Age Day 10   Moon Sign Gemini*

The focus is on being part of a group right now and drawing strength from the support that comes from others. This does not mean that you are always willing to co-operate and typical of your zodiac sign, you wish to remain first amongst equals. This fact might not suit everyone, and so a degree of diplomacy on your part is also called for.

17 SUNDAY ☿ *Moon Age Day 11   Moon Sign Cancer*

The argumentative side of your nature is highlighted now and this is partly thanks to the present position of the planet Mars in your solar chart. Try not to get involved in pointless debates about issues you cannot alter in any case. Better by far to get on well with everyone, because the help you need can be gained from surprising directions.

18 MONDAY ☿ *Moon Age Day 12   Moon Sign Cancer*

For the moment you can afford to be open-minded and quite democratic in your attitude. Your enthusiasm is apparent and you would willingly work alongside others in order to achieve a common goal. Speaking of goals, sporting activities could be much to the fore and you can make use of a high degree of energy right now.

19 TUESDAY ☿ *Moon Age Day 13   Moon Sign Leo*

The influence of the Moon in your chart today assists you to be enthusiastic and far from sensitive in your dealings with the world at large. Apparent insults are like water off a duck's back and you can laugh at yourself much more than would normally be the case. Why not get fully involved in fun pursuits?

20 WEDNESDAY   *Moon Age Day 14   Moon Sign Leo*

You can make this a good time socially. Venus has now moved into your solar eleventh house, and winning over others ought to be fairly simple. You can display a great deal of personal charm and will be high in the affections of people who don't usually give you a second glance. Actually, they might notice you much more than you think.

21 THURSDAY   *Moon Age Day 15   Moon Sign Leo*

Be prepared to simplify routines and create an environment that is geared towards plans for the future. At the same time save an hour or two to spend with family members. If you are always busy, you might sometimes forget the simple needs of people who you take for granted. A kind word or two can be very important.

22 FRIDAY   *Moon Age Day 16   Moon Sign Virgo*

In a social sense you can remain pretty much the centre of attention. Indeed, some of the compliments you can attract may be distinctly romantic in nature and might even lead to a slightly embarrassing situation. A day to avoid loud and contentious types, otherwise you could find yourself getting involved in an argument.

23 SATURDAY   *Moon Age Day 17   Moon Sign Virgo*

There are signs that before today is out one or two issues will rise to the surface and may seem far more important than they deserve. The fact is that the lunar low is on the way and this encourages a more contemplative frame of mind. If you can't make the progress you would wish, why not simply jog along for the next few days?

24 SUNDAY   *Moon Age Day 18   Moon Sign Libra*

You can easily alienate others unless you make a real point of letting them know you are listening to what they have to say. It's like taking a driving test. You know that you looked into your rear view mirror all the time, but the examiner didn't. You have to make everything more apparent in order to succeed during the lunar low.

25 MONDAY
Moon Age Day 19   Moon Sign Libra

A time of introspection is on offer and a period during which you can carefully evaluate your roles in life generally. Don't try to move any mountains at the moment because you would have trouble with molehills. By tomorrow you can get most aspects of your life back to normal and running smoothly.

26 TUESDAY
Moon Age Day 20   Moon Sign Scorpio

You will need to co-operate fully if you want to resolve problems. For this you can thank that most active of planets – Mars. In some situations you could be quite touchy, but not if you take the time to think things through well. This is not a good time for firing from the hip, and circumspection is definitely your best approach.

27 WEDNESDAY
Moon Age Day 21   Moon Sign Scorpio

Trends become more positive today and you enter a period during which it should be much easier to get ahead in a social sense. Active and enterprising, you can now show the true Aries face to the world at large. That's important because people respond very positively to your own certainty and to your decisive nature.

28 THURSDAY
Moon Age Day 22   Moon Sign Scorpio

What an excellent time this would be to plan a trip out somewhere. Of course you might be tied down with work, but if your time is your own, today would be right for ringing the changes. Rather than arguing about issues that are of no real importance, be prepared to save your powers of communication for issues that you know will become vital.

29 FRIDAY
Moon Age Day 23   Moon Sign Sagittarius

Leap year day offers an opportunity to get as many things organised as you can. Your usual thirst for new projects could be taking a back seat, simply because you want everything to be right as it stands. Others might think you are dragging your feet, so it is also important to explain yourself at every turn.

March 2008

1 SATURDAY
Moon Age Day 24   Moon Sign Sagittarius

Emotional outbursts are possible at the beginning of March, and once again the planet Mars is the culprit. Don't misplace your aggression, and even if it's difficult to avoid speaking your mind, you need to be careful regarding the recipient. Confidence shouldn't be lacking and in fact could be too great at times.

2 SUNDAY
Moon Age Day 25   Moon Sign Capricorn

When it comes to getting things done today you might prefer to rely on your own judgement and efforts. It isn't that you mistrust other people, but you know they can't do things the way you can. You might have to invent jobs for those around you if you don't want to offer any unintentional offence.

3 MONDAY
Moon Age Day 26   Moon Sign Capricorn

There could be some slight uncertainty today. The Sun is presently in your solar twelfth house and so the part you have to play in the wider world may not be quite as influential as you would wish. You might have to defer to the wishes of other people, and that never goes down very well with the typical Aries subject.

4 TUESDAY
Moon Age Day 27   Moon Sign Capricorn

Support can be gained from friends, and their mere presence in your life could stimulate some interesting ideas that you can put into practice later. This is also a good time for the romantically inclined Aries. You should be able to show your sensitive side and to think up the most endearing words of love.

5 WEDNESDAY   *Moon Age Day 28   Moon Sign Aquarius*

A day to avoid unnecessary assumptions and jumping to the wrong conclusions at home. Even if you are jogging along nicely at work, it may be relatives who present you with one or two problems just now. It would be best today to stick with your friends as much as proves to be possible.

6 THURSDAY   *Moon Age Day 29   Moon Sign Aquarius*

Trends bring the possibility of being led up the garden path by another individual. As a rule Aries is the most astute of all the zodiac signs, but just at present you may not exactly be firing on all cylinders when it comes to your natural intuition. If you must sign documents today, make sure you have read them fully.

7 FRIDAY   *Moon Age Day 0   Moon Sign Pisces*

You can make this a fairly light-hearted sort of day and a time during which your natural sense of humour is very much to the fore. You can't expect everyone to be laughing all the time, but when it matters the most you can get people to join in. Don't be too quick to apportion blame if something minor goes wrong.

8 SATURDAY   *Moon Age Day 1   Moon Sign Pisces*

If you are unsure about your goals and objectives at the moment, this would be a good time to stop and take stock. Things could become much more hectic across the next couple of days, whereas at the moment there should be time for reflection. A day to get plenty of rest and to avoid taking on jobs that are not your responsibility.

9 SUNDAY   *Moon Age Day 2   Moon Sign Aries*

The Moon returns to your zodiac sign, bringing with it the lunar high for the month. Now you can get fully in gear and can move forward on as many fronts as proves to be possible. With the Sun occupying your solar twelfth house you would still be well advised to take on jobs one at a time and to make sure things get finished.

10 MONDAY   *Moon Age Day 3   Moon Sign Aries*

Your judgement is well starred today and you shouldn't have any difficulty discovering that you can turn life to your distinct advantage. If it seems as though everyone around you is particularly friendly, the fact is that you are probably putting out just the right sort of messages yourself. Now is a time to ask for something important.

11 TUESDAY   *Moon Age Day 4   Moon Sign Taurus*

You would be wise to avoid taking too many financial risks, at least until after the 20th of the month. It's time to consolidate as far as cash is concerned – if only because you might come unstuck and make a fairly big mistake. When it comes to buying things you now ought to ask yourself in each case – 'Do I really need that?'

12 WEDNESDAY   *Moon Age Day 5   Moon Sign Taurus*

You may desire freedom but it's a commodity that may not be easy to find in the midst of many responsibilities. There ought to be at least part of the day you can call your own, and you might well choose to find a little corner where you can be alone. This twelfth-house period will soon be over, but for now, why not just chill?

13 THURSDAY   *Moon Age Day 6   Moon Sign Gemini*

Venus stands with the Sun in your solar twelfth house and that can mean a certain amount of minor drawbacks when it comes to your love life. Maybe you are not dealing with your lover in the right way, or it could simply be that there are different ideas about and you are finding it rather difficult to compromise right now.

14 FRIDAY   *Moon Age Day 7   Moon Sign Gemini*

You might still have some slight difficulty when it comes to getting your ideas across to others, but not half so much if you stop to think about matters first. There are positive qualities to your life at the moment. Not least of all you have scope to make new friends and may well also be taking on new responsibilities at work.

15 SATURDAY
Moon Age Day 8   Moon Sign Cancer

Intuition can be a powerful tool, and especially so for you at the present time. It would take someone extremely clever to pull the wool over your eyes, and you can show yourself to be astute for others, as well as for yourself. You needn't take no for an answer regarding an issue that has been uppermost in your mind, but do try to compromise.

16 SUNDAY
Moon Age Day 9   Moon Sign Cancer

Today's influences assist you to be more philosophical about your life in a general sense and to let things wash over you that caused real concern earlier in the month. This might be the first time this year that you begin to look around yourself and to realise that the world is waking from its winter sleep. Perhaps it's time for some fresh air!

17 MONDAY
Moon Age Day 10   Moon Sign Cancer

Today you can be particularly great when it comes to expressing yourself. For this you can thank the present position of the Moon, and you can exploit the tendency for all you are worth. In social situations you have what it takes to shine, and as the Sun nears the end of its twelfth-house journey for you, you can afford to let your more forceful side show.

18 TUESDAY
Moon Age Day 11   Moon Sign Leo

Where your love life is concerned you may need to be paying significant attention to what others are saying. This can be difficult, because although it is important to monitor the way your lover is feeling, this is not a time during which you should listen to gossip. Don't be afraid to turn on that intuition and follow your own hunches.

19 WEDNESDAY
Moon Age Day 12   Moon Sign Leo

You could be rather sensitive to criticism at the moment, and would be wise to curb your natural tendency to fire back if you think you are under attack. Most people are genuinely trying to be constructive on your behalf – a fact you might realise once you have had time to think things through. A circumspect attitude works best.

20 THURSDAY   *Moon Age Day 13   Moon Sign Virgo*

Now you are able to deal positively with a past issue, and your ability to look ahead becomes better than has been the case for some weeks. Attitude is especially important in your working life, and you might even be asked to take on some task that looks difficult. Don't worry – present trends help you to cope with it.

21 FRIDAY   *Moon Age Day 14   Moon Sign Virgo*

The current emphasis is on effort, and for many Aries people work remains a singular and important focus ahead of the weekend. The lunar low is about to arrive so no matter how much you commit yourself to practical matters, there's a chance something could go wrong. The weekend could be quiet, but you can make it happy.

22 SATURDAY   *Moon Age Day 15   Moon Sign Libra*

What you get from today and tomorrow depends entirely on the attitude with which you approach both days. You can't expect to have everything the way you would wish, but if you are willing to relax and to take life in your stride, you can be quite content with your lot. You can persuade others to rally round to lend a hand when it is necessary.

23 SUNDAY   *Moon Age Day 16   Moon Sign Libra*

Why not use today as a lay-off between major developments and be willing to plan ahead, though without putting in too much effort? Don't be too quick to take offence at remarks made by others, since they may not be for your ears in the first place. A newcomer to your life could offer a little light relief at some time today.

24 MONDAY   *Moon Age Day 17   Moon Sign Libra*

With the power of the Sun now in your zodiac sign, even the remnants of the lunar low are hardly likely to hold you back this week. There is far more enthusiasm available and a greater willingness to get involved in things. With everything to play for you probably need a good plan of action this week, especially at work.

25 TUESDAY   *Moon Age Day 18   Moon Sign Scorpio*

Trends enhance your ability to get down below the surface of situations and to see the motivations at their centre. Once again it is very important to use your intuition and to make decisions according to instinct. It seems you can get the world on your side for most of the time, and new possibilities are on offer all around you.

26 WEDNESDAY   *Moon Age Day 19   Moon Sign Scorpio*

Domestic matters would benefit from some thought. It could be that family members are behaving in a less than typical way, but the real problem is more likely to come from the direction of your partner. There is a good deal of excitement possible, maybe because of an event that is just around the corner. Why not join in the fun?

27 THURSDAY   *Moon Age Day 20   Moon Sign Sagittarius*

You would be wise to avoid routines at all cost because they are almost certain to get on your nerves at this time. It would be far better to take on a dozen different tasks today than to allow yourself to become bored. Aries can really fire on all cylinders now, bringing joy to your own life and to that of others, simply by being yourself.

28 FRIDAY   *Moon Age Day 21   Moon Sign Sagittarius*

Dealings with others offer you scope to use your most persuasive skills to get people to follow your will. You achieve this by a degree of persuasion, but also because it seems to those around you that your mind is working at full strength. The more certain you are of yourself, the greater can be your natural magnetism.

29 SATURDAY   *Moon Age Day 22   Moon Sign Sagittarius*

Even if a relationship issue gives you pause for thought, it needn't be allowed to get in the way of what is a very progressive period. If anything, you may be expecting just a little too much from yourself, and could afford to take a few hours to think matters through. Taking a trip with your partner, family members or friends might work wonders.

30 SUNDAY   *Moon Age Day 23*   *Moon Sign Capricorn*

Now you can accomplish feats that will surprise not only those around you but also you yourself. If you happen to work at the weekend, today ought to be excellent for pleasing yourself and for making progress simply because you know what to do and say. Be prepared to mesmerise superiors with your confidence and poise.

31 MONDAY   *Moon Age Day 24*   *Moon Sign Capricorn*

Dominating and coercive attitudes are to be avoided, particularly in your home environment. What might not help situations at all is if those around you are feeling competitive and argumentative too. Stick to friends and colleagues if you can today because in their company you are far less likely to go off at the deep end.

April

2008

1 TUESDAY
Moon Age Day 25   Moon Sign Aquarius

The first day of a new month assists you to be highly motivated, unusual in your thought processes and attitudes and eager to get on with things. Even if not everyone around you has the same idea, when it matters the most you can get your own way. Home-based matters should be easier today and you can let romance shine out noticeably.

2 WEDNESDAY
Moon Age Day 26   Moon Sign Aquarius

Venus remains in your solar twelfth house and demonstrates at the moment just how self-sacrificing you can be. You can afford to work long and hard in order to support a family member or a friend, and might even go against your better judgement in order to back them up. This is genuine loyalty and is one of your major strengths.

3 THURSDAY
Moon Age Day 27   Moon Sign Pisces

Right now you have an opportunity to transcend the everyday world and enjoy a distinctly meditative spell, as the Moon passes through your solar twelfth house. Even if you are still ready to take on the world, much of it seems to pass you by for the next couple of days. A little daydreaming is to be welcomed.

4 FRIDAY
Moon Age Day 28   Moon Sign Pisces

You have potential to be innovative when it comes to leadership issues, but at the same time you can take a low-key attitude to most aspects of life. Don't be too willing to put yourself out for anyone who has proved to be unreliable in the past, and listen carefully to your inner voice when it comes to taking financial risks. They may be a bridge too far.

5 SATURDAY
Moon Age Day 29   Moon Sign Pisces

Although you start today with the Moon in your solar twelfth house, it soon passes into your first house and also into the zodiac sign of Aries. There is more dynamism available now than you have experienced since the start of the year, and there is little doubt that you can persuade others to trust you to do just about anything that takes your fancy.

6 SUNDAY
Moon Age Day 0   Moon Sign Aries

Trends help you to reach your most creative, but you shouldn't allow your imagination to run away with you. A positive attitude is fine and so is a fertile mind but be realistic, and stick mainly to what you know. If you strengthen your finanaces you can afford to take the odd chance that you wouldn't have taken before.

7 MONDAY
Moon Age Day 1   Moon Sign Aries

The Moon remains in your zodiac sign and the lunar high encourages you to have a go at almost anything! There are signs that you are up for a good time and that you will be more than popular with others. Utilise this grand opportunity and make sure that you ask for anything that has been on your mind for quite a while.

8 TUESDAY
Moon Age Day 2   Moon Sign Taurus

You have the power to attract strong affection at the moment and it comes not only from expected but also quite unexpected directions. Being an Aries subject you are sometimes too busy to notice the way the wind is blowing with regard to the way you affect others. Even a virtual stranger may have a crush on you now!

9 WEDNESDAY
Moon Age Day 3   Moon Sign Taurus

Though you could be spending more than you might wish at the moment, a lot depends on the way you view situations. You must ask yourself whether the money you are shelling out is really bringing you the sort of value you expect. It could be that habit is playing a part in the way you deal with expenses. It's worth having a look.

10 THURSDAY   *Moon Age Day 4   Moon Sign Gemini*

It would be sensible to listen to what is being said around you at present. Even if you don't usually indulge in gossip or take much notice of it, it's a fact that you can gain from doing so at the moment. Routines could well get on your nerves and this is definitely a time for breaking the bonds of the normal and for seeking something new.

11 FRIDAY   *Moon Age Day 5   Moon Sign Gemini*

You need to look out for sudden possibilities that can lift your life somewhat and add to the potential excitement surrounding you. There are gains to be made on the financial front, though probably not as a result of what would usually be termed good luck. You make your own luck under present trends, and the results are obvious.

12 SATURDAY   *Moon Age Day 6   Moon Sign Cancer*

A time for imagination and for stretching credibility is now at hand. You need to reach into the deeper recesses of your mind and to see possibilities that pass others by. The weekend ought to offer you the chance to get away from routines, and you would be quite mad to turn down the opportunity of doing something exciting.

13 SUNDAY   *Moon Age Day 7   Moon Sign Cancer*

Current influences encourage you to shun rules and regulations in favour of simply doing what takes your fancy. That also means lifting the lives of people around you. There should be time to spend with family members and at the very least you can lift the spirits of your partner and let them know why they are with you.

14 MONDAY   *Moon Age Day 8   Moon Sign Leo*

You now have more energy at your disposal, and a definite idea about how you are going to use it in order to better your lot generally. The Sun remains in your solar first house and allows you to stretch the boundaries of the possible, whilst at the same time showing the world at large what an Aries subject is really all about.

15 TUESDAY *Moon Age Day 9 Moon Sign Leo*

There can be a lack of good communication in your vicinity, though you can make sure this isn't down to you. All the same it's worth putting in that extra bit of effort that can make all the difference. Be willing to stand up for what you believe, and particularly so if the welfare of someone you care for is on the line.

16 WEDNESDAY *Moon Age Day 10 Moon Sign Virgo*

Everything now conspires to bring out the best in you and also those with whom you have a close attachment. If ever there was a time for love, this is it. Make it clear how you feel, especially if you are trying to impress someone who is not an item in your life yet. You have the power to sweep just about anyone off their feet.

17 THURSDAY *Moon Age Day 11 Moon Sign Virgo*

Today is a time during which you can look for and expect encouragement from others. This is especially the case at work, and is a response on their part to the very real effort you have put in previously. Don't worry too much about spurious aches and pains around now. In the main you can keep yourself quite healthy.

18 FRIDAY *Moon Age Day 12 Moon Sign Libra*

It would be a good idea today to slow down and to allow things to take their own course for a couple of days. The lunar low does nothing to boost your vitality, and even if you do try to do something important, there may be delays and disappointments. Why not put life on hold for a while and watch the flowers grow instead?

19 SATURDAY *Moon Age Day 13 Moon Sign Libra*

The lunar low is still around so this may not be the most remarkable weekend you have ever experienced. You are now easily defeated and might not be able to see your own potential in the way you normally do. Your best approach is to rely on the good offices of those around you and let your partner or family members take some of the strain.

20 SUNDAY   *Moon Age Day 14   Moon Sign Libra*

A phase of financial improvement is now available. The first part of the day might remain rather lacking in anything special, but Mercury is in your second house and you can soon improve things. Once the Moon moves from Libra, it's up and away for Aries. Don't take no for an answer regarding an issue that is uppermost in your mind.

21 MONDAY   *Moon Age Day 15   Moon Sign Scorpio*

It is now possible for you to give your finances a definite lift. The Sun moves today from your solar first to your solar second house, and although this takes away some of the dynamism that has been present, it replaces this with better powers of discrimination and a shrewder attitude. For the next month or so you can also show your intuitive side.

22 TUESDAY   *Moon Age Day 16   Moon Sign Scorpio*

At the moment you have scope to be a natural diplomat and it shouldn't be at all hard for you to find the right words that act as oil on troubled waters. It isn't necessarily that you are causing problems yourself but you turn your abilities towards sorting out issues created by both colleagues and friends.

23 WEDNESDAY *Moon Age Day 17   Moon Sign Sagittarius*

This is a good time for using new information that you find, probably in some fairly unusual places. The fact is that if you are keeping your eyes and ears wide open, you will be in the best possible position to do what is necessary to turn situations to your own advantage. For the moment you can also take routines in your stride.

24 THURSDAY   *Moon Age Day 18   Moon Sign Sagittarius*

Trends assist you to attract the sorts of things that please you and to do the same job for those you love. Romance is on the cards at the moment and you shouldn't find it difficult to have the right words to sweep someone off their feet. Young or young-at-heart Aries subjects could well be embarking on a new romance now.

25 FRIDAY   *Moon Age Day 19   Moon Sign Sagittarius*

With Venus now in your solar first house a period of less pressure and more contentment is on offer. Aries is always striving for something, but it is possible that some of your usual efforts don't seem quite so important for a while. With this period also comes a chance for greater relaxation and an ability to look deep inside yourself.

26 SATURDAY   *Moon Age Day 20   Moon Sign Capricorn*

You could well become somewhat restless and a little bored with existing routines, and although this is not a time during which you would break out big time, it's worth putting small changes into action. These might not be much at all but the bearing they have on your life in the longer-term is quite apparent.

27 SUNDAY   *Moon Age Day 21   Moon Sign Capricorn*

A productive period is at hand regarding material and financial issues. The arrival of Sunday probably offers you more time to think and also a few moments to look through documents that have a bearing on your financial stability. It is even possible that you will find yourself to be better off than you previously thought.

28 MONDAY   *Moon Age Day 22   Moon Sign Aquarius*

Do keep a lookout for old faces at the start of this week. It is possible that someone you knew well is now back in your vicinity, and if it is someone you really liked before, don't be afraid to strike up a relationship once again. Even if things aren't exactly the way they used to be, you can recreate at least a few of the good times that are gone.

29 TUESDAY   *Moon Age Day 23   Moon Sign Aquarius*

Relationships can now be boosted by your powers of communication and by a desire on your part to get your message across intact. You know the right things to say and will take the necessary time to say them. There is probably no real rush at the moment, and you can make that a positive thing for all sorts of reasons.

30 WEDNESDAY   *Moon Age Day 24   Moon Sign Aquarius*

Personal matters can affect your capabilities in the outside world and the pull of the past still remains strong – maybe too strong in some ways. You need to be particularly realistic in your view of situations out here in the middle of this week, and shouldn't allow sentiment to cloud your judgement. A day to keep a sense of proportion regarding money.

May

2008

1 THURSDAY
Moon Age Day 25   Moon Sign Pisces

There could be some profitable developments on offer, and for this you can thank the planet Venus, which has now passed into your solar second house. Perhaps a little financial luck is available, but it's far more likely that you are simply in a better position to make things work out the way you would wish.

2 FRIDAY
Moon Age Day 26   Moon Sign Pisces

Before the end of today the Moon returns to your zodiac sign, but at the start of the day there may well be a few limitations in your path. What matters is the way you approach these. Your best response is not to take no for an answer and to be fully in the mood to do whatever is necessary to get ahead.

3 SATURDAY
Moon Age Day 27   Moon Sign Aries

The lunar high is at hand and you can make this weekend both bright and exciting. Don't be tied down by routines and do whatever is necessary to get your own way. This isn't selfish, particularly if you are doing your best for others on the way. Any project that has been on the go for some time can now be brought nearer to completion.

4 SUNDAY
Moon Age Day 28   Moon Sign Aries

New financial propositions are available, and it shouldn't be hard for you to turn these to your advantage. Your potential level of good luck is probably off the scale, though this shows itself in some rather peculiar ways. A day to make room for change and for travel, and if possible choose this time to take a journey that is simply for fun.

5 MONDAY
Moon Age Day 0   Moon Sign Taurus

More financial options should become available to you around this time. You are able to look at life in a slightly different way and can be flexible in your approach to most situations. This is not at all the sort of time during which you should set your face in any specific direction – especially if that means losing your own choices.

6 TUESDAY
Moon Age Day 1   Moon Sign Taurus

Even if you are still well on target for getting things done, you might have to contend with one or two people who seem to be working against your best interests. Actually they could simply be trying to help, so it would be sensible not to lose your temper. It appears that you can get even usually nosey and interfering types on your side now.

7 WEDNESDAY
Moon Age Day 2   Moon Sign Gemini

Mercury is now in your solar third house and this encourages a definite and quite obvious inquisitiveness that is greater than usual in your case. You now have scope to find out not only that things work, but also how they function. The exercise might slow you down somewhat but at least you can satisfy your curiosity.

8 THURSDAY
Moon Age Day 3   Moon Sign Gemini

Domestic issues might seem to be an area that demands your attention more than usual. Perhaps someone else is away from home or refusing to pull their weight for some reason. No matter what the cause, you may decide to roll up your sleeves and get stuck in with the general chores more than is usually the case.

9 FRIDAY
Moon Age Day 4   Moon Sign Cancer

Business affairs are favoured at this time, and you can make significant progress, even if you have to think harder than usual in order to find the right answers. This shouldn't bother you at all, particularly if you are in the right frame of mind for a challenge. Be prepared to forge new friendships around now.

101

10 SATURDAY
Moon Age Day 5   Moon Sign Cancer

You can now take advantage of a faster pace of life than has been the case for some time. Aries is really on a roll and because of this you may feel able to take on a dozen different jobs at the same time. Be careful that you don't overtax yourself, and make sure that everything is done to the best of your ability.

11 SUNDAY
Moon Age Day 6   Moon Sign Leo

There are some good social boosts around on this spring Sunday and you will need to move pretty fast to keep up with all of them. If the suggestions that others make about how you should spend your free time accord with your own opinions, you may decide to go with the flow for a good deal of today. It's not worth getting tied down to routines.

12 MONDAY
Moon Age Day 7   Moon Sign Leo

You can make sure that money isn't too much of an issue at the start of this week, and indeed the planetary line-up indicates that you could be just a little better off than you expected. Maybe it's as a result of actions you took in the past, or it could simply be that Lady Luck is shining on you to a greater extent than was the case earlier.

13 TUESDAY
Moon Age Day 8   Moon Sign Virgo

New prospects for change do exist, even if you have to work rather hard to worm them out. Your curiosity is still highlighted, and you can use it to look deep into the workings of life. Others may find you to be slightly more intense than usual, and that means having to explain yourself to a greater extent.

14 WEDNESDAY
Moon Age Day 9   Moon Sign Virgo

Even if you want to make yourself as useful as possible today, the only trouble could be that you don't know how best to proceed. It might be sensible to ask others what they really need and to react accordingly. This is no time to be in the dark, and you only have to open your mouth in order to understand some issues better.

15 THURSDAY   *Moon Age Day 10   Moon Sign Virgo*

With the Moon speeding towards your opposite zodiac sign of
Libra, things could be quietening down a little. This leaves you with
more moments in which to ruminate on life and specific situations.
This may not be the most exciting day of the month, but it does
carry opportunities for genuine rest and for positive introspection.

16 FRIDAY   *Moon Age Day 11   Moon Sign Libra*

It might seem as though bad luck is attending your actions at
present, but in reality you are only entering a short phase during
which you need to charge flagging batteries. If you don't push
yourself too hard, you can make the most of a time during which
others are willing to take the strain. Why not enjoy the ride for once?

17 SATURDAY   *Moon Age Day 12   Moon Sign Libra*

There are signs that it is very difficult for you to get out of the habit
of being in charge of everything. If you are still not as positive as
usual, that means once again allowing others to make the running.
Following in the wake of some genuinely good ideas won't do you
any harm, and might give you new incentives.

18 SUNDAY   *Moon Age Day 13   Moon Sign Scorpio*

If you were sensible across the last couple of days you now have
scope to emerge into a place in life that should be both comfortable
and more certain than might have been the case earlier in the
month. You should be well rested and now anxious to start pushing
forward again. Romance in particular can be fortunate at this time.

19 MONDAY   *Moon Age Day 14   Moon Sign Scorpio*

Any positive information that comes your way at this time should be
turned to your advantage. This is particularly true at work, and
progress could well be the result. When necessary you can change your
way of thinking and should find it easy to respond to any requests that
are coming your way from superiors or those in overall authority.

20 TUESDAY
Moon Age Day 15   Moon Sign Scorpio

There are definitely new opportunities around that allow you to broaden your horizons in some way. All new incentives should be grabbed with both hands, and there is little doubt that you would benefit at present from any opportunity to travel. Stretching your mind should be appealing, and you won't hesitate to really turn on your intuition.

21 WEDNESDAY
Moon Age Day 16   Moon Sign Sagittarius

A day to look to colleagues and associates to boost your ego. Your nature is charming and you should be particularly good in social situations. If you have been seeking to sweep a particular person off their feet, this is the time to do so. There is very little around you now that could be considered negative.

22 THURSDAY
Moon Age Day 17   Moon Sign Sagittarius

You should certainly benefit now from a broader range of interests and from as much variety as possible. It doesn't really matter if you are having to deal with a host of different situations at the same time because you are more than capable of multi-tasking under present planetary trends. Friends could be especially warm.

23 FRIDAY
Moon Age Day 18   Moon Sign Capricorn

As you review certain accomplishments you may decide that a little fine-tuning is necessary. That's fine, but you also have to remember that the more you tamper with issues that have already been sorted, the greater is the chance they will go wrong. Don't be afraid to keep faith with your original decisions and wait patiently for the results.

24 SATURDAY
Moon Age Day 19   Moon Sign Capricorn

A time of optimism and communication is definitely on offer. The Sun is now in your solar third house, bringing that part of the year when you are encouraged to talk to anyone. If you are called upon for an opinion you won't be stuck, and public speaking could be the easiest thing in the world for you now.

25 SUNDAY   *Moon Age Day 20   Moon Sign Capricorn*

A time of high ego energy is indicated, not only because of the position of the Sun but also on account of Mars, which is now in your solar fifth house. The only slight problem is that you might not have quite enough sympathy for the situations others find themselves in. Try to stretch your imagination and your empathy if possible.

26 MONDAY   *Moon Age Day 21   Moon Sign Aquarius*

Personal dealings with loved ones might even be described as idyllic at the present time, so you can make sure your home life is going rather well. People can now be persuaded to offer you the best of what they are, and that encourages you to share the best of yourself with them. All in all this could be a fairly exceptional week.

27 TUESDAY   ☿ *Moon Age Day 22   Moon Sign Aquarius*

You can now seek out interesting people just about anywhere you go – and they won't always be individuals you have known in the past. New friendships are possible, some of which are forged in quite surprising circumstances. New interests are on offer, at least one of which might become a virtual obsession.

28 WEDNESDAY ☿   *Moon Age Day 23   Moon Sign Pisces*

A slight withdrawal is now possible, brought about as a result of your present twelfth-house Moon. This is not at all a bad thing because you have a few hours during which you can think things through rather carefully. Don't be so quick to rush to judgements today, but rather understand that life is filled with shades of grey.

29 THURSDAY   ☿ *Moon Age Day 24   Moon Sign Pisces*

Another slightly quieter day is on offer, but once again you can afford to be content with your lot and more than willing to wait and see. This can be a great time of year and you may well have sufficient time on your hands right now to take a pleasant walk. Nature is waking more and more, which ought to delight you.

30 FRIDAY ☿ *Moon Age Day 25   Moon Sign Aries*

Let's hope you did relax on Wednesday and Thursday because there may be little time to do so now! The lunar high inspires you to be more positive and go-getting than is usually the case, even for Aries. Don't take no for an answer today. If there is something you really want, make it your own, and be prepared to ask others for help.

31 SATURDAY ☿ *Moon Age Day 26   Moon Sign Aries*

Today you could discover that getting your own way is as easy as falling off a log. You shouldn't have to push anyone because such is the power of your personality that you can simply ask them to fall in line with your requests. Money should be easier to come by and there are indications that your love life will be especially rewarding.

June

2008

1 SUNDAY
☿ *Moon Age Day 27   Moon Sign Taurus*

At the start of a new month the pace of life may not be quite so frenetic, and so there should be time to compose yourself and to look at the bigger picture in most situations. Your expectations should now be more realistic and you can afford to wait for some of your plans to materialise. Romance is once again well starred.

2 MONDAY
☿ *Moon Age Day 28   Moon Sign Taurus*

The communications you have with others today should contribute to an easier path through life generally for all concerned. If you are specific and concise in what you are saying, you should leave nobody in any doubt that you understand situations well. Even if not everyone you meet is equally lucid, you can allow for that fact too.

3 TUESDAY
☿ *Moon Age Day 29   Moon Sign Gemini*

Opportunities present themselves at the moment to get your ideas across to people who really count. Trends suggest that you are filled with good ideas and that you want to do everything you can to make them into realities. There may be moments when you fail to be quite as patient as is necessary, but that's Aries!

4 WEDNESDAY
☿ *Moon Age Day 0   Moon Sign Gemini*

This is yet another day during which your powers of communication are put to the test. It doesn't matter who you are talking to and what you are talking about, the important thing is that you are interacting with the world at large. There's probably no shyness about Aries at the moment, though it's a rare situations when there is.

5 THURSDAY ☿ *Moon Age Day 1 Moon Sign Cancer*

Your strength lies in getting your family, friends and colleagues to pull on your behalf at the moment, which is why you should find June to be one of the most useful months of the year so far. You shouldn't lack resourcefulness and can easily think up new strategies, both for yourself and on behalf of others.

6 FRIDAY ☿ *Moon Age Day 2 Moon Sign Cancer*

A day to put some of that famous Aries versatility to use now, particularly out there in the bigger world. This is not really a time for concentrating on domestic issues, but rather a period during which you need to show those who are in charge just how capable you can be. At the same time you need to have fun, so why not plan a special evening?

7 SATURDAY ☿ *Moon Age Day 3 Moon Sign Leo*

The Moon is now in your solar fifth house – a good place for personal expression. As a result you can make this weekend one of constant contact with others and a period during which you are hardly likely to withdraw into your shell. Attitude is everything when it comes to explaining a sensational idea to others.

8 SUNDAY ☿ *Moon Age Day 4 Moon Sign Leo*

You may now encounter one or two arguments and could get involved in a fairly competitive phase when dealing with friends. This might resolve itself to sporting activities of one sort or another, and if you do indeed take part in any team game or individual pursuit it is important to remain as fair-minded as possible.

9 MONDAY ☿ *Moon Age Day 5 Moon Sign Leo*

Aries is now potentially more argumentative than will have been the case in the recent past. That's fine if you really need to make your position known, but the problem is that you could lose your temper over issues that are of no real importance. Be prepared to curb your emotions a little and constantly put yourself into the other person's shoes.

10 TUESDAY ☿ *Moon Age Day 6 Moon Sign Virgo*

The main emphasis today is on work and the way you interact with the world at large in a professional sense. If you are between positions at the moment or actively looking for another, now is the time to concentrate most of your efforts. Those Aries people who are settled at work can make this a time for advancement.

11 WEDNESDAY ☿ *Moon Age Day 7 Moon Sign Virgo*

Things could well slow down somewhat as today grows older, so if there is anything that really needs to be done, it's worth concentrating your efforts near the start of the day. The reason for the change in events is the arrival of the lunar low, and this month it can really take the wind out of your sails. Some extra patience is called for.

12 THURSDAY ☿ *Moon Age Day 8 Moon Sign Libra*

Professional dealings can be difficult, particularly if you don't have quite the drive and enthusiasm that so typifies your nature as a rule. Do your best to be calm, cool and collected, whilst at the same time being willing to let others make some of the running. The very best course of action for you today and tomorrow is to rest.

13 FRIDAY ☿ *Moon Age Day 9 Moon Sign Libra*

It's a good job that most Aries people are not superstitious, because this month your lunar low coincides with Friday the 13th. Even if there are moments when you wish you had stayed in bed, you can still make some progress, especially in a personal and a romantic sense. There could well be some real personalities about now.

14 SATURDAY ☿ *Moon Age Day 10 Moon Sign Scorpio*

The lunar low is now out of the way and with little Mercury so well placed in your solar third house you can be at your most persuasive whenever it matters the most. Confidence to do the right thing remains high and you shouldn't be stuck for an answer, no matter how much life and circumstance seems to put you on the spot.

15 SUNDAY ☿ *Moon Age Day 11* *Moon Sign Scorpio*

If you want to make fundamental changes to your life at the moment, Sunday should offer you the chance to do so – if only in your mind at first. Although you are a person who often reacts instinctively, you can also be a deep thinker, and it probably benefits you at the moment to mull things over before taking action.

16 MONDAY ☿ *Moon Age Day 12* *Moon Sign Scorpio*

You can turn the start of this working week into an enjoyable time of expanding freedom, simply by being yourself and by enjoying the interaction you have with the world at large. It is possible that romance will be especially well highlighted for many Aries subjects at this time, and there could also be some happy surprises.

17 TUESDAY ☿ *Moon Age Day 13* *Moon Sign Sagittarius*

You now seem to have a real knack for getting others on your side and can do much to put them into an agreeable mood. However, you probably won't achieve this by bombarding them with so many ideas and possibilities that they become dizzy. 'One thing at once' is the right adage for today, both for yourself and on behalf of the world at large.

18 WEDNESDAY ☿ *Moon Age Day 14* *Moon Sign Sagittarius*

Trends suggest that your love life may be characterised at the moment by a tendency to argue about issues that are really of very little importance. It would be better by far to avoid discussing contentious issues altogether because when you do there is a tendency for you to become slightly domineering and less inclined to listen.

19 THURSDAY ☿ *Moon Age Day 15* *Moon Sign Capricorn*

This has potential to be a fairly secure period during which you can make steady progress towards your chosen objectives. All the same you may decide to work alone for at least some of the time because your tendency to co-operate successfully is not at all strong. The same is not true at home, where family members can prove to be a real joy.

20 FRIDAY
☿ *Moon Age Day 16   Moon Sign Capricorn*

There is now a greater focus on your home and family. This is influenced by the movement of the planet Venus into your solar fourth house, where it will remain for a week or two. An ideal day to spend time with loved ones and to get in touch with a family member who lives at a significant distance.

21 SATURDAY
Moon Age Day 17   Moon Sign Capricorn

This is a much better time for get-togethers and discussions that have a bearing on your future in connection with relatives, and especially your partner. It could be that you are planning holidays or maybe deciding about a change of house. Whatever you are talking about, you can make sure that there will be a good consensus.

22 SUNDAY
Moon Age Day 18   Moon Sign Aquarius

Your home environment, friends and surroundings in general are especially highlighted at this phase of the month. Most of what you are doing should be harmonious and you won't be upsetting the applecart as can sometimes be the case for the dominant Aries subject. Most people find you to be warm and caring.

23 MONDAY
Moon Age Day 19   Moon Sign Aquarius

You can afford to relax and take care of yourself today, even if you feel under pressure with regard to your work. Standing back and taking stock will be very worthwhile and there is little reason to rush any situation for the moment. If people want to confide in you, it is important to give them the time they need to talk.

24 TUESDAY
Moon Age Day 20   Moon Sign Pisces

There is just a slight possibility that the things you do today will have to be redone tomorrow, so you need to exercise more care than usual. It isn't that you are prone to making practical mistakes, but is more the case that you may be subject to faulty thinking before you even start any particular task. Don't be too quick to make up your mind.

25 WEDNESDAY   *Moon Age Day 21   Moon Sign Pisces*

Communication is clearly the key to success and you are now much more able to get things right first time. It's possible that you are slightly quieter than usual, but you can put that fact down to the position of the Moon, which is presently in your solar twelfth house. Many Aries subjects will be seeking a little isolation at present.

26 THURSDAY   *Moon Age Day 22   Moon Sign Pisces*

Another slightly quieter day is on offer, but it comes just ahead of the lunar high, so the time to take stock should be very welcome and can even prove to be rewarding. There may be some issues around that you will simply have to think through for yourself, particularly if there isn't the level of support about that you might wish.

27 FRIDAY   *Moon Age Day 23   Moon Sign Aries*

Along comes the lunar high, once again assisting you to be filled with energy and determination. You can be creative, inspirational and good to know. There is excitement available, and most of it is created by you. If people love to have you around, you can be the life and soul of any party that is taking place.

28 SATURDAY   *Moon Age Day 24   Moon Sign Aries*

There need be no lack of generosity on your part when it comes to dealing with other people. This weekend can offer a distinctly exciting period and a time when it would be a terrible waste of time to simply sit around at home. Why not get out of the house and enjoy yourself in the company of people who stimulate your mind?

29 SUNDAY   *Moon Age Day 25   Moon Sign Taurus*

Trends suggest that in love you need to seek a state of harmony and to scrupulously avoid self-centred indulgence. When Aries is at its most generous it is the most amazing zodiac sign of all, and right now you need to give the best of impressions. This is partly true because you have no idea who is paying attention and watching you closely.

30 MONDAY   *Moon Age Day 26   Moon Sign Taurus*

The start of this working week would be a great time for gathering information, ahead of a new push of some sort. Current plans may well be under discussion and you at least need to let colleagues and friends think that you are taking their opinions into consideration. Someone quite surprising could be knocking at your door soon.

July

2008

1 TUESDAY
Moon Age Day 27   Moon Sign Gemini

It's the first day of a new month and you have scope to demonstrate a great sense of enjoyment and a desire to break the bounds of the normal. There could hardly be a better time than this for Aries to take a holiday, but if that isn't possible simply make the best you can of your free moments – some of which might be spent with your lover.

2 WEDNESDAY
Moon Age Day 28   Moon Sign Gemini

A day when you can get things generally to unfold just as you would wish them to do – though you do need to take care that plans are constantly nudged in the right direction. You can't afford to leave anything to chance if you want to be successful, and extra work could be called for. New information can be gleaned from colleagues.

3 THURSDAY
Moon Age Day 0   Moon Sign Cancer

This may prove to be a time of greater emotion on your part. For this you can thank the present position of the Moon, which also encourages you to be closer to your home and family. People you don't see too often may be uppermost in your mind, and making contact in some way could work wonders.

4 FRIDAY
Moon Age Day 1   Moon Sign Cancer

Ambitious ideas can be brought to the fore today, and even if you are champing at the bit to put them into practice, there are certain practicalities that will have to be dealt with first. A few tedious jobs can be dealt with quite quickly, but if you rush things too much you will have to repeat some of your actions time and again.

5 SATURDAY
Moon Age Day 2   Moon Sign Leo

This is likely to be a good time for leisure and pleasure pursuits and not a period during which you should be giving too much thought to work. All work and no play can make Aries a dull boy or girl, and the weekend offers you the chance to relax. Even extending yourself physically is OK, as long as it isn't for practical reasons.

6 SUNDAY
Moon Age Day 3   Moon Sign Leo

Domestic matters are well starred, and it should be possible now to get others to willingly do things for you. It isn't that you are lazy but there just seems to be so much to get done. You can still find time for personal enjoyment and should do your best to make a real fuss of your partner at this time.

7 MONDAY
Moon Age Day 4   Moon Sign Virgo

There is a more definite focus on getting things done at the start of this new working week. If not everyone appears to be pulling their weight, you might decide it is easier for you to do things yourself than to chivvy them along. Aries is in the mood for seeing results, and that means getting on with it.

8 TUESDAY
Moon Age Day 5   Moon Sign Virgo

A day to remain very motivated, particularly when it comes to your own life. Your need for a greater sense of personal security is likely to be strong and at the same time you could show yourself to be quite sentimental. For once Aries seems quite vulnerable, which is something others might tend to exploit somewhat.

9 WEDNESDAY
Moon Age Day 6   Moon Sign Libra

Beware of taking too many risks today. The lunar low is around and it's worth being slightly more careful than usual. From a physical point of view your body is in a regenerating phase, so you can't expect to be quite as energetic as usual. You can still achieve plenty, but need to do so in a generally low-key sort of way.

10 THURSDAY   *Moon Age Day 7   Moon Sign Libra*

There could be a few disappointments about at present and your best approach is simply to be patient. Nothing that happens to you today is likely to be more than temporary in its influence, and a few worries turn out to be nothing more than mirages. The more you relax, the easier this phase of your month should be.

11 FRIDAY   *Moon Age Day 8   Moon Sign Libra*

You start today with the lunar low still around, but this isn't a situation that lasts very long. By the early afternoon you can get right back on form, anxious to show the world at large that you are really on the ball and filled with a much greater series of expectations regarding your own capabilities.

12 SATURDAY   *Moon Age Day 9   Moon Sign Scorpio*

This is a time during which dumping anything that is no longer of any use to you can work wonders. This doesn't simply apply to that ancient computer or redundant kitchen utensil, because it also relates to outmoded ideas and opinions. It's time for a spring-clean in every sense of the word, even if that is a little uncomfortable.

13 SUNDAY   *Moon Age Day 10   Moon Sign Scorpio*

This would be a good day for spending some time at home and being on your own for a while if at all possible. The Sun is now in your solar fourth house and this does tend to encourage introspection. At the same time if there are things that need to be said to a family member, this might be as good a time as any.

14 MONDAY   *Moon Age Day 11   Moon Sign Sagittarius*

You can benefit well from social relationships under present trends, particularly if you are in the market to make new friends. People from the past who emerge into your life again may bring with them a nostalgic but generally pleasant period. There are signs that Aries cannot help being sentimental at the moment.

15 TUESDAY   *Moon Age Day 12   Moon Sign Sagittarius*

Mars is now in your solar sixth house and this could allow a real split in your personality. Whilst you may be quite committed to home and family and showing yourself to be very sensitive, at work you can push harder than has been the case for quite a while. Not everyone will find your sudden changes in persona easy to deal with.

16 WEDNESDAY   *Moon Age Day 13   Moon Sign Sagittarius*

Professional schemes can help you to achieve excellent results, and you are so self-assured that other people may be constantly turning to you for help and support. Your insights and initiatives can be an inspiration to all manner of folk, though there may be some who fail to trust you at all.

17 THURSDAY   *Moon Age Day 14   Moon Sign Capricorn*

Family issues are still highlighted, offering you scope to commit yourself to domestic matters more than to anything else. It could be that you see the way forward in terms of making your home more comfortable, or it is just possible that you are weighing up the pros and cons of a house move.

18 FRIDAY   *Moon Age Day 15   Moon Sign Capricorn*

Not everything you want to achieve will be possible straight away. Some patience is necessary and it would be sensible to itemise your requirements, in order that you can prioritise your efforts. It's worth calling on the support of someone who is really in the know and seeking their assistance in at least one of your plans.

19 SATURDAY   *Moon Age Day 16   Moon Sign Aquarius*

Romantic interests are where it's at for many Aries subjects today. This is a period during which you should feel freer to express your true feelings – even if that means laying your emotions open for someone else to view to a much greater extent than would normally be the case for Aries. You should be happy with the result.

20 SUNDAY
Moon Age Day 17   Moon Sign Aquarius

Mercury is now in your solar fourth house and this should certainly help you to bring out the livelier aspects of your nature, particularly when you are in your home environment. Chances are you don't work at the weekend but if you have to, this would be a really good day to rely on someone who is in charge.

21 MONDAY
Moon Age Day 18   Moon Sign Aquarius

Trends suggest that you want to do things your own way and won't take kindly to others interfering in what you see as your own affairs. This will be especially true if the people concerned hardly know you at all. Nevertheless, you need to keep your temper because this is not a good period for going off at the deep end.

22 TUESDAY
Moon Age Day 19   Moon Sign Pisces

A period of increased personal magnetism is on offer, and this helps you to use your powers of attraction where others are concerned. You might see this as a good thing, but for some Aries subjects it can be a double-edged sword. You have no control over who pays you more attention and that might inspire jealousy in someone else.

23 WEDNESDAY
Moon Age Day 20   Moon Sign Pisces

Be prepared to move things quicker in your life as a whole, as it could appear as if the winds of change are blowing right now. You can thank the lunar high that begins to show its influence in the afternoon and which helps you to be far more dynamic and determined to push forward. Do your best not to make adversaries now.

24 THURSDAY
Moon Age Day 21   Moon Sign Aries

This has potential to be an easy sort of day and a time when it is clear that things are running in your favour. Now is the time to take the initiative in career situations and when it comes to more personal situations don't be afraid to speak your mind. If ever there was a time to sweep someone off their feet, this is the right moment for Aries.

25 FRIDAY
Moon Age Day 22   Moon Sign Aries

This can be a time of interesting and exciting changes. The end of the working week might be quite welcome, but probably not because you are tired. On the contrary you could be champing at the bit to do something that simply pleases you and this evening is likely to offer the right moment. Warmth and support can be sought from friends.

26 SATURDAY
Moon Age Day 23   Moon Sign Taurus

Your charm shouldn't be in doubt and neither should your determination. It isn't hard to make the best possible impression this weekend and to persuade someone you care about that you are fully committed to them. Aries has scope to be more romantic now than at any time so far this year. What a great time this would be to take a holiday.

27 SUNDAY
Moon Age Day 24   Moon Sign Taurus

At work it is important to develop a compromise with others but this being a Sunday, you may not have such matters on your mind. In personal attachments you are able to take the lead and even if you show yourself to be charming, approachable and committed, you need leave nobody in any doubt about your role as a leader.

28 MONDAY
Moon Age Day 25   Moon Sign Gemini

There are new and better ways to express yourself at the moment, but you have to look around in order to find them. You need to remain as original as possible because you can get people to notice you more if you break a few taboos. Even if you are not setting out to shock the world, it won't do any harm to make yourself better known.

29 TUESDAY
Moon Age Day 26   Moon Sign Gemini

In a practical sense it is possible that you have a sense of impatience with certain people who won't or can't do things the way you would wish. At the same time you are still able to display your originality to a great extent and won't be put into any sort of mould. This should make for an interesting if somewhat strange sort of day.

30 WEDNESDAY   *Moon Age Day 27   Moon Sign Cancer*

If you feel that something is missing today, it may be because you are not keeping yourself fully up to date with local and national events. You may have been concentrating so hard on your own lot in life that you have failed to appreciate what is happening just outside your door.

31 THURSDAY   *Moon Age Day 28   Moon Sign Cancer*

A day to stand up for anyone who is in trouble and be willing to put forward their point of view, even if it doesn't necessary coincide with your own. It does you good to see things from a different perspective and it is also important that you champion those who don't have your self-assurance or ability to speak publicly.

August

2008

1 FRIDAY
Moon Age Day 0   Moon Sign Leo

The first day of August offers you a chance to get on a winning streak, especially when it comes to charm and to the favourable impression you can make on others. Making your mark in social situations shouldn't be difficult and you can mix freely with many different sorts of people. Friends seek you out avidly at this time.

2 SATURDAY
Moon Age Day 1   Moon Sign Leo

There ought to be more than enough room in your daily agenda for having fun and for doing things that have no useful or financial part to play in your life. Today is a time for letting go of some of the responsibility and for becoming a child again. There can be great joy in your life, and you have to find ways to express it.

3 SUNDAY
Moon Age Day 2   Moon Sign Virgo

Even if lots of energy is still going into getting things done, the focus is still on having fun and helping others to enjoy themselves. This ought to be a holiday and even if you have to work you can make it into a sort of vacation. Avoid getting waylaid by any issues that mean you having to be all grown up and clever.

4 MONDAY
Moon Age Day 3   Moon Sign Virgo

This is a time during which there is plenty of romantic energy available. It doesn't matter whether you are eighteen or eighty, you can still feel the pull of deep affection and the need to express your feelings. Be prepared to put yourself on stage at present and to find the right audience under differing circumstances.

5 TUESDAY
Moon Age Day 4   Moon Sign Virgo

The pace of life could be slowing somewhat as the Moon moves ever closer to your opposite zodiac sign of Libra. It's time to rest a little more and to rely on the good offices of those around you. Not that you will slow down altogether because that is not the Aries way. New hobbies could be on offer now.

6 WEDNESDAY
Moon Age Day 5   Moon Sign Libra

Today responds best if you keep an even pace and don't take on any more work than is strictly necessary. It's worth allowing others to do some of the more tedious jobs and delegating whenever you can. In the meantime you can find ways to sit back and enjoy yourself – recharging those flagging Aries batteries whilst others put in more effort.

7 THURSDAY
Moon Age Day 6   Moon Sign Libra

There are more promising ideas around at work for many Aries subjects just now, but you might find it difficult to benefit too much from them whilst the lunar low is still around. Why not watch and wait, at least until tomorrow? By then you can put yourself in a better position to put in that extra effort that can make all the difference.

8 FRIDAY
Moon Age Day 7   Moon Sign Scorpio

You can now afford a lighter, brighter mood, and probably won't mind in the least if someone seems to be questioning your way of doing things. You have what it takes to show great patience and to be an excellent teacher at the moment, whilst still pushing steadily towards your own objectives. Family members can be a real source of joy at present.

9 SATURDAY
Moon Age Day 8   Moon Sign Scorpio

Trends assist you to demonstrate a great insight into the way others are behaving and this is especially true as far as your friends are concerned. You needn't judge anyone, but will simply be in a good position to offer either the right advice or practical help when it matters the most.

10 SUNDAY   *Moon Age Day 9   Moon Sign Sagittarius*

You have potential to expand your social life and to enjoy deep discussions with all manner of people. New friends could be the result, even if for most of this year you will rely primarily on people you have known for a long time. You can be high in the popularity stakes and won't find it difficult to get others to follow your quite natural lead.

11 MONDAY   *Moon Age Day 10   Moon Sign Sagittarius*

You would be wise to avoid impatience at the start of this working week. Mars is still in your solar sixth house and encourages pushiness on occasions. However, other planetary positions testify to the common sense in sitting back and watching for a few days. Something you didn't want to do might easily become irrelevant.

12 TUESDAY   *Moon Age Day 11   Moon Sign Sagittarius*

In practical discussions today you can show your quick-witted, funny and engaging side. At home things may be a little fraught, though probably not as a result of any circumstance created by you. Younger people especially can be a cause of some minor frustration and need dealing with carefully.

13 WEDNESDAY   *Moon Age Day 12   Moon Sign Capricorn*

Your ability to see both sides of almost any situation is quite noteworthy around now and you are subject to fairly inspirational ideas when it matters the most. Today has potential to be entertaining and filled with promise for those Aries subjects who are able to grasp new situations quickly.

14 THURSDAY   *Moon Age Day 13   Moon Sign Capricorn*

You may decide to enjoy a little romance today and there is a definite chance of an emotional release. Some of the gains you can make around now could come like a bolt from the blue, but if you are naturally quick on the uptake you won't turn down any chance of a lucky break. All the same this is not a good time for gambling.

15 FRIDAY　　　*Moon Age Day 14　　Moon Sign Aquarius*

There is absolutely no doubt that you can handle bigger responsibilities at this time, so you shouldn't be afraid to stretch the bounds of the credible in order to prove yourself to others. Actually you probably won't have to because all you have shown yourself to be in the recent past will be enough.

16 SATURDAY　　　*Moon Age Day 15　　Moon Sign Aquarius*

Teamwork issues could be marred by disagreements. This trend could show itself in almost any sphere of your life, all the way from work to sporting activities. Why not take some time out this weekend to simply do what takes your fancy? You are a naturally hard worker but like every other human being you need periods to enjoy yourself.

17 SUNDAY　　　*Moon Age Day 16　　Moon Sign Aquarius*

This can be a period of detachment and quiet, and a time during which you decide to take on much less in the way of direct responsibility. By the end of today the Moon will be passing through your solar twelfth house and that assists you to show a much more emotional face to the world at large.

18 MONDAY　　　*Moon Age Day 17　　Moon Sign Pisces*

Although life may still be short on actual action, this would be a very good day during which to talk and plan with those who are in higher positions than you are. Like all Aries people you have what it takes to reach the top of the tree eventually but for the moment you might have to listen carefully to what others are suggesting.

19 TUESDAY　　　*Moon Age Day 18　　Moon Sign Pisces*

The Sun is now presently in your solar fifth house and your romantic feelings are much accentuated under present trends. You can find the right words to express your feelings and shouldn't be held back by embarrassment. Family members probably do need your support around now, even if you can't really understand why.

20 WEDNESDAY   *Moon Age Day 19   Moon Sign Aries*

There is no such thing as a sense of proportion whilst the lunar high is around. Today and tomorrow are your days, and mark the time during August when you can be at your most dynamic and potentially successful. If you get Lady Luck on your side at the moment you can afford to take the odd chance.

21 THURSDAY   *Moon Age Day 20   Moon Sign Aries*

Your strength lies in appearing to the world at large to be very much at ease right now, and indeed that is the truth. You show a good attitude when dealing with others and shouldn't be stuck for an idea all day. This would be a great time to take a holiday, and if you are already on vacation you can make this a really excellent time.

22 FRIDAY   *Moon Age Day 21   Moon Sign Taurus*

Things could slump a little if you find yourself beset with practical problems, and maybe have no real way to sort them out immediately. Patience is called for – plus the assistance of someone who is clearly in the know. Don't be too inclined to assume that anything has been done correctly. It is important for you to check.

23 SATURDAY   *Moon Age Day 22   Moon Sign Taurus*

Even if you are now involved in a harder-working period than was the case earlier in the month, you can relish the fact that you are so often able to take charge. The hours may be long but the sense of satisfaction can be much greater and that is what so often counts for Aries. There might not be a great deal of time for emotional responses today.

24 SUNDAY   *Moon Age Day 23   Moon Sign Gemini*

On the ideas front you probably need to be careful about moving ahead too quickly. Be prepared to test things out carefully and don't put too much effort in any direction unless you know that you will turn a profit of some sort. Of course this doesn't apply to your personal life, but even here you would be wise to exercise a little care.

25 MONDAY
Moon Age Day 24   Moon Sign Gemini

If you now have something rather irritating to do, your best approach is to get it out of the way as early in the day as proves to be possible. It is likely that a change of attitude is called for when it comes to dealing with a strictly practical matter. You might also have to eat a little humble pie, which isn't easy.

26 TUESDAY
Moon Age Day 25   Moon Sign Gemini

This can be a favourable period for all domestic issues and for making family business livelier and more rewarding. You can afford to let others have their head to a greater extent than might sometimes be the case. Even if your trust is slightly misplaced, it is necessary to allow younger people especially to find their own way in life.

27 WEDNESDAY
Moon Age Day 26   Moon Sign Cancer

You have scope at work to get everything running quite smoothly – leaving you to please yourself to a much greater extent. New diversions are a possibility and you might be looking for some alterations to your social life, in order to allow time for new interests. This is not a day when you are likely to run out of steam quickly.

28 THURSDAY
Moon Age Day 27   Moon Sign Cancer

Trends assist you to bring an important relationship fully into focus today. There could be some tension when it comes to making compromises, particularly if you are not in the right frame of mind to do so. Keep up your efforts to streamline your social life, otherwise you are going to tire yourself out completely!

29 FRIDAY
Moon Age Day 28   Moon Sign Leo

Getting your own way with others is largely a matter of charm at the moment. Some firm support becomes available, most likely at work, but it is also obvious that your social conscience is heightened under present trends. If there is something happening in the vicinity of your home that you don't like, take the time to speak out.

30 SATURDAY   *Moon Age Day 29   Moon Sign Leo*

Work issues are likely to be boosted, though of course this won't be significant to Aries subjects who either don't work or are away from work at the weekends. You are still in a position to have a good time and to show your best possible face to social situations. Don't be surprised if you make yourself extra-popular at present.

31 SUNDAY   *Moon Age Day 0   Moon Sign Virgo*

You can work wonders today when it comes to simply communicating with others. Finding the right words to express yourself is rarely difficult, but it might be suggested that you can be positively inspirational at the moment. Someone you see quite rarely might be making a repeat appearance to your life very soon.

September

2008

1 MONDAY
Moon Age Day 1   Moon Sign Virgo

You may find this an especially good day to be talking to people who have some real influence. There are gains to be made simply by being in the right place at the best possible time, and Aries looks especially good in all discussions about money – particularly how to get more of it.

2 TUESDAY
Moon Age Day 2   Moon Sign Libra

If all of a sudden it seems as though the wind is taken out of your sails, you can blame the arrival of the lunar low. Don't be too quick to take on anything new and before you embark on any sort of adventure you should ideally wait for a day or two. Why not take the chance on offer at the moment to get some real, solid rest?

3 WEDNESDAY
Moon Age Day 3   Moon Sign Libra

Your options might seem somewhat limited right now but that is mainly because of the present position of the Moon. All the same it would be wise not to push your luck too much and to wait until tomorrow before you really get adventurous. In your mind at least you can be very inventive and well able to plan ahead.

4 THURSDAY
Moon Age Day 4   Moon Sign Scorpio

It seems that romance is well starred for Aries. Those of you who are already attached can strengthen your relationship, whilst Aries people who have been looking for new love should keep their eyes wide open at present. Attitude is all-important when dealing with people who have proved awkward in the past.

5 FRIDAY
Moon Age Day 5   Moon Sign Scorpio

With a little extra effort you can find good ways to improve your lot, especially on the home front, but you might not be able to have too much of a bearing on the way friends and family are actually behaving. It would probably be better not to try, and to simply enjoy the originality that stands around you on all sides.

6 SATURDAY
Moon Age Day 6   Moon Sign Scorpio

Trends now assist you to seek invaluable assistance from others, no matter how much or how little you have to do with them. It just seems that people want to help you out and to give you that extra little nudge towards success whenever it seems to be possible. A day to keep an eye open for romance because the prognosis is good now.

7 SUNDAY
Moon Age Day 7   Moon Sign Sagittarius

Concentrating and getting down to some really essential ideas now becomes possible as the Sun stands strong in your solar sixth house. Time is likely to be on your side when it comes to plans that are slowly but definitely maturing, and you have what it takes to turn heads, especially when in social situations.

8 MONDAY
Moon Age Day 8   Moon Sign Sagittarius

There ought to be a good opportunity to do your own thing today and plenty of chance to make the best of impressions when you are dealing with others. Socially speaking you can be on good form and will probably want to mix and mingle as much as possible under present trends. Not absolutely everyone might applaud your efforts however.

9 TUESDAY
Moon Age Day 9   Moon Sign Capricorn

There are signs that your partner, or maybe a family member, is especially bossy at the moment, and if you like to be in charge of most situations yourself, that's not something you take to well. Nevertheless you should let them have their head for the moment, because in some way that you don't understand it's very important to them.

10 WEDNESDAY   *Moon Age Day 10   Moon Sign Capricorn*

If you can see ways to turn situations to your advantage at the moment, you needn't hold back when it comes to tinkering with situations of many different sorts. Fine-tuning is what today is all about, though you also have to realise that in at least one situation only a completely new start is likely to do the trick.

11 THURSDAY   *Moon Age Day 11   Moon Sign Capricorn*

Helpful experiences are now possible as a result of friendships today, and you can afford to rely heavily on your friends, one or two of whom show themselves to be as loyal and kind as always. Show your appreciation to them and to any family members who are putting themselves out for you.

12 FRIDAY   *Moon Age Day 12   Moon Sign Aquarius*

There are signs that you will have your work cut out simply keeping on top of material priorities today, so there may not be as much time as you would wish to spend with either your partner or close family members. All the same you do have a tongue in your head, and even a word or two uttered at the right time can offer reassurance.

13 SATURDAY   *Moon Age Day 13   Moon Sign Aquarius*

Keep your eyes open today because you have scope to make some interesting contacts with people who are definitely in a position to do you some good. These may be individuals you already know but are just as likely to be complete strangers. You needn't be backward when it comes to expressing an opinion at the moment.

14 SUNDAY   *Moon Age Day 14   Moon Sign Pisces*

If someone now requires extra patience and understanding from you, that might mean putting yourself out a great deal on their behalf. Chances are this will be a person who has shown great consideration to you in the past and so you won't mind at all doing all you can to support them or to do something practical for them.

15 MONDAY   *Moon Age Day 15   Moon Sign Pisces*

Although trends highlight your considerate side at the moment, you also have to realise that it might be difficult to please all of the people, all of the time. Some individuals won't care what you do and will still expect more. The planetary line-up encourages concentration on one job at once under present trends.

16 TUESDAY   *Moon Age Day 16   Moon Sign Aries*

Now the Moon returns to your zodiac sign of Aries, bringing the lunar high for September with its focus on excitement and determination. If there is a fly in the ointment it could be that you are trying to achieve too many things. It might not be a bad thing to itemise your wishes and to do first what seems most credible.

17 WEDNESDAY   *Moon Age Day 17   Moon Sign Aries*

Success is within your grasp at the moment, no matter what you decide to undertake. Inspiration is available, and you should follow your gut reactions in most situations. Money may be easier to come by, even if this turns out to be as a result of efforts you put in a good deal earlier. Why not spend some time with friends and enjoy yourself?

18 THURSDAY   *Moon Age Day 18   Moon Sign Aries*

For the third day in a row the Moon occupies your zodiac sign and you can still make sure you're on top form. Popularity is there for the taking, and this is a time to shine socially. If you don't have anything specific planned for the evening, you might decide to invite friends out. You need company and gain from it.

19 FRIDAY   *Moon Age Day 19   Moon Sign Taurus*

The time is right to plan ahead for bigger things in the material sphere. Maybe you are looking at the possibility of a change in your career or perhaps thinking about a change of abode. Whatever is on your mind, you have what it takes to think big under present astrological trends and needn't be held back by cautious types.

20 SATURDAY   *Moon Age Day 20   Moon Sign Taurus*

Success is, in the main, now closely related to the way you get on with other people. There may be certain individuals about at the moment who can do you a great deal of good. The problem might be recognising who they are, particularly if not every one of them is an individual you either like or spend much time with as a rule.

21 SUNDAY   *Moon Age Day 21   Moon Sign Gemini*

Right now you can make the most of a potentially hectic phase. Apart from preparing for new plans and getting on with practical jobs at home, others may need your help and support. Finding time to fit everything in might not be easy and you will need to compartmentalise your day in order to live up to expectations.

22 MONDAY   *Moon Age Day 22   Moon Sign Gemini*

You value a personal approach right now and that turns out to be a good thing. Trends suggest you can't deal with anything at a distance and will be much better when face to face with others. Bringing a family member round to your point of view could be the most difficult job of the day, but you can take that in your stride too.

23 TUESDAY   *Moon Age Day 23   Moon Sign Cancer*

Friends could now prove to be more reliable than relatives. Even a virtual stranger has what it takes to sum you up and it might surprise you to realise how closely someone has been watching you. It is possible that you are now being earmarked for advancement, and if this is the case you need to believe that you deserve it.

24 WEDNESDAY   *Moon Age Day 24   Moon Sign Cancer*

This is a period for positive self-expression and for being willing to speak your mind, even if you know there are people around who are bound to disagree. Bear in mind that there are some individuals who would argue that black was white just for the sake of the discussion. You will be more respected if you say what you think.

25 THURSDAY ☿ *Moon Age Day 25   Moon Sign Leo*

With Venus now in your solar eighth house it is possible that you will be able to make some slight gains in the financial stakes. Maybe an amount of money comes your way unexpectedly or is related to something you have forgotten about. Either way, it would be rather silly of you to look a gift horse in the mouth.

26 FRIDAY ☿ *Moon Age Day 26   Moon Sign Leo*

It's worth getting colleagues to put you firmly in the social mainstream, particularly if you are now getting on better at work. Mixing business with pleasure is something Aries people often do and can be especially beneficial under present astrological trends. In conversations you simply need to be yourself.

27 SATURDAY ☿ *Moon Age Day 27   Moon Sign Virgo*

Now that the Sun occupies your solar seventh house you have scope to get on extremely well in partnerships or in any sort of twosome. This isn't always the case with Aries, which has a tendency to go it alone, but for the moment you share well and enjoy the exercise. For some there could be a very strange bedfellow about to emerge.

28 SUNDAY ☿ *Moon Age Day 28   Moon Sign Virgo*

The focus is on your great desire to take control, even in partnerships. This is such a natural tendency for Aries that it will always show through unless you keep a strict control of your own nature. Being in command is fine, just as long as everyone agrees that this is the best way forward. At least be open to discussion.

29 MONDAY ☿ *Moon Age Day 29   Moon Sign Libra*

Along comes the lunar low, a time when you might decide to take some rest and to allow others to make the running for a day or two. This doesn't mean that you have to retire into the background in every situation. You merely need to recharge your personal batteries and to take stock of situations for a few hours.

30 TUESDAY ☿ *Moon Age Day 0 Moon Sign Libra*

It's the last day of September and you could still feel rather lacking in energy and more inclined than usual to take a back seat. Don't expect too much from life and if possible sit in a corner with a good book and enter a different world for a while. No matter how much you push, it will be hard to break down certain barriers today.

October

2008

1 WEDNESDAY ☿ *Moon Age Day 1 Moon Sign Libra*

As October gets underway the Moon still occupies the zodiac sign of Libra, but not for long. In a social sense at least today could be mentally uplifting and might offer you the opportunity to pit your wits against someone you both like and respect. Clashing antlers can be a real mark of respect in the case of Aries people.

2 THURSDAY ☿ *Moon Age Day 2 Moon Sign Scorpio*

You are well able to cut through red tape today and probably won't take at all kindly to people who overcomplicate situations of any sort. If getting down to the real task at hand is something you are anxious to do, and you are unlikely to take no for an answer when you know that more is possible. This is Aries at its best.

3 FRIDAY ☿ *Moon Age Day 3 Moon Sign Scorpio*

Trends assist you to get into the good books of people who are in an excellent position to do you a real favour. However, today is not all about practicalities but has a very good social feel too. A new romance could be on the cards for some Aries people – maybe even if you had not expected it to happen.

4 SATURDAY ☿ *Moon Age Day 4 Moon Sign Sagittarius*

It is through co-operation that you stand the best chance of getting things done this weekend, so you need to curb your natural tendency to hand out orders all over the place. If you allow others their head they can be of great use and can even cope with certain jobs better than you could. Nobody can be good at everything, not even you!

5 SUNDAY   ☿ *Moon Age Day 5   Moon Sign Sagittarius*

Communication and travel are well accented. Your intuition should be greatly improved at this time and you have a great desire to seek out the wide blue yonder. If you had been considering a late holiday you could hardly choose a better time than this, though even a short break or a day away from routines would be welcome.

6 MONDAY   ☿ *Moon Age Day 6   Moon Sign Sagittarius*

Social pleasure can now be integrated into your overall plans for the week. This is a good time to mix business with pleasure and to get satisfaction from both. You can begin new friendships this week and also get a positive response from people who are in positions of authority. All in all a potentially positive period for Aries.

7 TUESDAY   ☿ *Moon Age Day 7   Moon Sign Capricorn*

This would be a good day for constructive career building and for planning ahead as far as your professional life is concerned. There could be a slight lull in romantic potential, particularly if you are busy doing other things. Try not to be too selective about jobs and sort out some of the less pleasant ones too.

8 WEDNESDAY   ☿ *Moon Age Day 8   Moon Sign Capricorn*

Right now you can afford to move away from the superficial and take a deep and thorough look at life. Whilst others graze the surface of situations you can get out your microscope if necessary in order to make certain that you understand. This kind of care should pay dividends in the end, even if some people laugh at you now.

9 THURSDAY   ☿ *Moon Age Day 9   Moon Sign Aquarius*

The social contacts you have been making of late can be of great use to you right now. This will be especially true in professional situations. Don't be too surprised if you are being sought out for special treatment from those in authority. You have what it takes to offer your opinion to someone close to home.

10 FRIDAY ☿ *Moon Age Day 10   Moon Sign Aquarius*

Relationship matters could be causing some slight anxiety around now, but you can ensure that this does not last long. For most of the time you can be easy-going and find that those with whom you mix during the day are just as relaxed as you are. This would be a good day to ask for a favour.

11 SATURDAY ☿ *Moon Age Day 11   Moon Sign Aquarius*

If there have been specific worries at the back of your mind, now is the time to dispel them like the morning mist. Rather than worrying them out of existence, ask yourself whether you were making too much of an issue of them in the first place. A feeling of significant relief could follow.

12 SUNDAY ☿ *Moon Age Day 12   Moon Sign Pisces*

With Mars in your solar fourth house there is a tendency now to feel quite emotional about certain issues. These situations are most likely to be associated with relationships of one sort or another, and your best response is to talk things through in order to settle your mind. Aries can be quite worrisome on occasion under present trends.

13 MONDAY ☿ *Moon Age Day 13   Moon Sign Pisces*

Stand by for a busier time, though not particularly for today. It's worth planning ahead, but without pushing yourself too much at the start of this working week. For most Aries people it will be enough to say what you want in order for others to do their best to see your plans mature. Make sure you have some good friends around you now.

14 TUESDAY ☿ *Moon Age Day 14   Moon Sign Aries*

The lunar high brings what has potential to be the most progressive phase of the month and offers you the chance to get ahead on a number of different fronts. Arrangements made today reflect your dynamic and go-getting frame of mind. You can now make those with whom you mix very envious of your charisma and potential success.

137

15 WEDNESDAY ☿ *Moon Age Day 15   Moon Sign Aries*

You have what it takes to get things to continue in a very positive way and to turn situations to your advantage, even without trying very hard. A combination of past efforts and present certainties allows you to glide towards your objectives, whilst appearing to be the coolest and most collected person around.

16 THURSDAY ☿ *Moon Age Day 16   Moon Sign Taurus*

The support you can now attract from others should be stronger at the moment than has seemed to be the case for quite some time. You can make the best use of this situation by relying on colleagues and good friends, whilst at the same time checking details and making certain that you are still fully in command of all situations yourself.

17 FRIDAY *Moon Age Day 17   Moon Sign Taurus*

You can afford to press on with your daily business, generally unconcerned about issues that are not really yours to sort out. If you get yourself tied down with worries that rightfully belong to other people, you will slow your own progress. It's fine to stand up for your friends, but beware of trying to live their lives for them.

18 SATURDAY *Moon Age Day 18   Moon Sign Gemini*

Venus, presently in your solar eighth house, contributes to you being a shrewd and calculating operator. Anyone would have to get up extremely early in the morning in order to pull the wool over your eyes at the moment. Generally speaking you know what you want from life and have a good idea how to go about getting it.

19 SUNDAY *Moon Age Day 19   Moon Sign Gemini*

This would be an excellent time to be on the move, and the chance of you making some real gains in the material world are extremely good. At the same time you should remember that this is a Sunday. The year is moving on towards its end and the weather won't be improving. All the more reason to get some fresh air and enjoy the great outdoors.

20 MONDAY
Moon Age Day 20   Moon Sign Cancer

Along comes a potentially demanding period and a time during which you may decide to buckle down to something you don't relish too much. Once you get started there should be little or no problem, but it could be the thought of unsavoury jobs that makes you feel a little uneasy at the start of this new working week.

21 TUESDAY
Moon Age Day 21   Moon Sign Cancer

Little Mercury, well placed in your solar chart, helps you to enjoy improved social and romantic possibilities around now. You can make sure your lifestyle is going more or less the way you would wish, and even if there are hiccups in personal attachments, in the main you should be quite content with your lot.

22 WEDNESDAY
Moon Age Day 22   Moon Sign Leo

There is a great deal in your chart now about self-expression, leisure and pleasure. All you need in order to make today go with a real swing is a good dose of optimism – together with the support of like-minded friends. Personal attachments can be strengthened and family members might actively seek your advice around now.

23 THURSDAY
Moon Age Day 23   Moon Sign Leo

It might not be what happens on the surface that really interests you today but rather the undercurrents of life. For once Aries becomes a deep thinker, you can turn your intuition up full. You can do yourself a great deal of good, both personally and professionally, by tuning in to what people are thinking rather than saying.

24 FRIDAY
Moon Age Day 24   Moon Sign Virgo

Right now it is important to take life one-step at a time and to avoid being overwhelmed if everything seems to be happening at once. Beware of biting off more than you can chew at work, and when you are at home allow relatives or your partner to do something on your behalf. This isn't the most energetic phase of the month for you.

25 SATURDAY — *Moon Age Day 25   Moon Sign Virgo*

If there was only one day during October when it would really benefit you to get a change of scenery, that day is today. Everything points to your need for an alteration in your routines and for the chance to look at something different – most favourably in the company of someone you either love or at least deeply admire.

26 SUNDAY — *Moon Age Day 26   Moon Sign Virgo*

Energy and enthusiasm may be low, and they won't get too much better for the next couple of days. Before today is out the Moon occupies the zodiac sign of Libra, bringing the lunar low as far as you are concerned. Your best response is to take life steadily, enjoy a laugh in the company of friends, but avoid pushing too hard towards any destination.

27 MONDAY — *Moon Age Day 27   Moon Sign Libra*

Expectations could now be slightly unrealistic, and it's worth being quite circumspect about what you plan to do in the near future. The lunar low offers you the opportunity to think about things more fully and a time during which you will be realistic – verging on pessimistic. This is not always a bad thing, as you should discover.

28 TUESDAY — *Moon Age Day 28   Moon Sign Libra*

Trends indicate some dissatisfaction with your work routines and with the way things are turning out as far as your social plans are concerned. Just remember where the Moon is and don't take either yourself or your life too seriously. This is also a time to think about leaving behind unnecessary baggage as you move forward in life.

29 WEDNESDAY — *Moon Age Day 0   Moon Sign Scorpio*

Now you begin to show real insight and your independent approach to life is both refreshing and useful. Not everyone might have your best interests at heart, but you do have what it takes to turn situations to your advantage, no matter what others might think. You have scope to dream up new and revolutionary ways to do tedious jobs.

30 THURSDAY   *Moon Age Day 1*   *Moon Sign Scorpio*

This is another good day for broadening your mental horizons and for showing the world at large just how capable you can be. Be prepared to vary your usual routines as much as possible and to stand up for yourself over any issue that means a lot to you. You might also be very protective of friends and inclined to argue on their behalf.

31 FRIDAY   *Moon Age Day 2*   *Moon Sign Sagittarius*

Emotional confrontations are probably best avoided today. There is a distinct possibility that you could get yourself involved in some sort of argument that will be both pointless and potentially destructive. When it comes to issues about which you have no real opinion, make it plain that you are willing to be flexible.

November

2008

1 SATURDAY
Moon Age Day 3   Moon Sign Sagittarius

The first day of November offers a chance to ring the changes again. Maybe it has only now occurred to you that there are only two months left in this particular year and that there are things you haven't done yet. Now is the time to get stuck in and to make a real splash socially, as well as pushing harder at work.

2 SUNDAY
Moon Age Day 4   Moon Sign Sagittarius

A little variety is worth a great deal at the start of November. Venus is now in your solar ninth house and this encourages you to look around more, with a sense of potential excitement and enthusiasm. Don't try to do everything at once but do make sure that you end today having achieved something – no matter how minor it may be.

3 MONDAY
Moon Age Day 5   Moon Sign Capricorn

You have what it takes to advance in professional developments, and to make a good impression on just about everyone you meet. Don't be fooled into thinking that someone knows better than you do about any aspect of your life, because you can be especially shrewd, calculating and in the know at present.

4 TUESDAY
Moon Age Day 6   Moon Sign Capricorn

You can apply your intuition to problem solving today and should have a good deal of fun on the way. There are areas of your life that might need improving, or else things you want to address out there in the world as a whole. Whatever you turn your mind to at present is grist to the mill of your curiosity.

5 WEDNESDAY   *Moon Age Day 7   Moon Sign Aquarius*

It looks as though under present trends you have scope to enjoy the company of a wide range of different sorts of people. You can show great charm and a willingness to take the other person's point of view on board a little more than would sometimes be the case. At work you may decide to find new avenues for your existing talents.

6 THURSDAY   *Moon Age Day 8   Moon Sign Aquarius*

Trends indicate that your instincts are well honed and your ability to look at others in a positive way has rarely been better. When dealing with awkward types you can develop just the right psychological approach and needn't be at all fazed when put on the spot in almost any sort of situation. This is a time when Aries can really shine.

7 FRIDAY   *Moon Age Day 9   Moon Sign Aquarius*

Relationships could seem to be just a little emotionally unstable for a day or two, though probably not as a result of anything you are saying or doing. Mars remains in your solar eighth house and although its position there has many favours to offer you, it can also shake the boat in terms of personal attachments.

8 SATURDAY   *Moon Age Day 10   Moon Sign Pisces*

As the Moon passes through your solar twelfth house you might actively choose to spend a little time ruminating about situations from the past and deciding on ways that your experiences can help in the future. You are also more inclined to be taking on some fairly quiet pastime or hobby – maybe alongside a friend.

9 SUNDAY   *Moon Age Day 11   Moon Sign Pisces*

A day to dream up something to do that pleases you exclusively. If you've done a great deal of thinking and acting on behalf of others during the last couple of weeks, you now deserve a treat yourself. Things could get very hectic at the start of next week, so why not take life steadily on this late autumn Sunday?

10 MONDAY

Moon Age Day 12   Moon Sign Aries

During November the lunar high coincides with the start of a new working week and helps you to catapult into all sorts of possibilities. Lady Luck should be truly on your side and you needn't be stuck for an idea or two. Now could be the best time of the month to take actions that lead to more money coming your way.

11 TUESDAY

Moon Age Day 13   Moon Sign Aries

This has potential to be a good day when it comes to problem solving and with regard to personal advancement. Now is the time to let those in positions of authority know how good you are, and to focus on new responsibilities. Whatever the demands, you are up for it and should be enjoying life.

12 WEDNESDAY

Moon Age Day 14   Moon Sign Taurus

You have what it takes to glean some profound insights today and to be very astute and even quite psychic. In a practical sense you need to dump outmoded concepts or efforts that have proven themselves to be a waste of time. Don't chase rainbows that you know are going to disappear as soon as you approach them.

13 THURSDAY

Moon Age Day 15   Moon Sign Taurus

Maybe you could afford to be just a little more ambitious and even manipulative at the moment. Of course you don't want to feel that you are manoeuvring people into positions that work to their disadvantage, but this is not what you will be doing. You can ensure that things you undertake now have positive repercussions for others.

14 FRIDAY

Moon Age Day 16   Moon Sign Gemini

Mars remains in your solar eighth house and you are still in a good position to dump anything that is either outmoded or devoid of any real use. Aries travels best when it travels light and that is certainly true in life at the present time. You may even be quite ruthless in your determination to get rid of anything unnecessary.

15 SATURDAY   *Moon Age Day 17   Moon Sign Gemini*

Following the same general pattern that has been obvious for a while, you can now afford to break ties that are no longer of any use to you and could be making new friendships all the time. The potential for romance is good and especially so for Aries people who are presently forming new attachments or formalising more casual ones.

16 SUNDAY   *Moon Age Day 18   Moon Sign Cancer*

You can make this a happy phase at home and create an especially caring and sharing sort of environment for yourself and your loved ones. The most pleasing moments you encounter today are likely to come along courtesy of family members and you show yourself to have more time than usual for domestic issues.

17 MONDAY   *Moon Age Day 19   Moon Sign Cancer*

A day to put your inner drive fully in gear. This should allow you to feel that you are improving in every possible way. This might lead you to a desire to remodel yourself even more, perhaps through diets or health regimes. If so you need to proceed carefully. In time you can achieve anything, but be steady.

18 TUESDAY   *Moon Age Day 20   Moon Sign Leo*

It looks as though success is there for the taking in just about anything you do at present, though you might be pushing yourself just a little too hard in some respects. In a few days the Sun will pass out of your solar eighth house, allowing you to feel somewhat more settled and content than seems to be the case now.

19 WEDNESDAY   *Moon Age Day 21   Moon Sign Leo*

Where future plans are concerned the presence of Venus in your solar tenth house at the moment gives you ample opportunity to plan ahead. This is particularly true with regard to your career, but it is also the case that you could be successfully negotiating travel plans that will mature at the other end of the coming winter.

20 THURSDAY   *Moon Age Day 22   Moon Sign Leo*

If you have an intimate issue on your mind at the moment, be prepared to get it sorted out before you move on to other matters. There are some small surprises in store at present and though most of these can be used to your advantage, you do need to be in a position to respond to situations quickly.

21 FRIDAY   *Moon Age Day 23   Moon Sign Virgo*

With a few distractions about now that Mars has moved into your solar ninth house, you may not be quite as clear-sighted as was the case only a few days ago. More care is necessary when dealing with personal issues, and trends could also hamper your ability to get things right first time – every time.

22 SATURDAY   *Moon Age Day 24   Moon Sign Virgo*

Your confidence could take something of a knock later on today, as the Moon moves into the zodiac sign of Libra. In the meantime you can jog along quite nicely, though it's not worth pushing yourself more than proves to be necessary. You can't be running at full speed all the time, and there is nothing wrong with ticking over.

23 SUNDAY   *Moon Age Day 25   Moon Sign Libra*

You needn't let the lunar low bother you in the slightest this month, unless that is you are determined to push forward in life no matter what the obstacles. There are times when the Aries individual works better when up against problems, but this is not one of them. Why not shelve contentious issues for a day or two and simply rest?

24 MONDAY   *Moon Age Day 26   Moon Sign Libra*

The continuing quiet perod might seem especially odd at the start of a new working week. Nevertheless there are gains to be made. Now is the time to watch, listen and wait. Almost anything that is taking place in your vicinity can be turned to your advantage and you can show yourself to be as astute as ever. Pay attention now, act later.

25 TUESDAY   *Moon Age Day 27   Moon Sign Scorpio*

Trends now stimulate the powerful desire to get things done that typifies your zodiac sign. The restrictions are out of the way and nothing need hold you back if you are certain of the direction you wish to take. It's worth paying attention to what your partner or a good friend is saying. If you do, you could save yourself a lot of effort.

26 WEDNESDAY   *Moon Age Day 28   Moon Sign Scorpio*

A little positive thinking on your part could bring some very happy experiences and should allow you to work positively towards a longed-for objective in a personal sense. You can persuade others to help you out at present and it is clear that you remain popular within almost any group. People might look to you for guidance now.

27 THURSDAY   *Moon Age Day 29   Moon Sign Scorpio*

A desire for personal freedom may now be so strong within you that you would do almost anything to avoid feeling fettered. There is nothing at all odd about this as far as you are concerned. The fact is that Aries needs space and can soon get very frustrated if it is restricted to places or situations that feel constraining.

28 FRIDAY   *Moon Age Day 0   Moon Sign Sagittarius*

You have what it takes to get career issues going your way and to make gains in a number of different potential directions. Remove obstacles from your path when it is possible to do so, but do also be willing to listen to the advice of someone who is an expert in their field and who does know better than you.

29 SATURDAY   *Moon Age Day 1   Moon Sign Sagittarius*

This is a fascinating day to be out and about rather than doing either boring or routine jobs. If your time is your own it's worth finding some way to get out and about, most rewardingly in the company of someone you love to be with. The evening could offer interesting social possibilities, as well as some new sort of diversion.

30 SUNDAY
Moon Age Day 2   Moon Sign Capricorn

Current influences highlight a slightly argumentative side to your nature that could lead to a few spats within the family. Some of your former tolerance for the strange behaviour of others is now missing and that could mean you will react more quickly. Try to remain cool, whatever happens.

December

2008

1 MONDAY
Moon Age Day 3   Moon Sign Capricorn

It will probably occur to you today that this is the first of December and so therefore Christmas is only a few short weeks away. Maybe that's a good thing because you are not the sort of person who does best by planning for things like holidays months ahead. You can make today steady and fruitful.

2 TUESDAY
Moon Age Day 4   Moon Sign Capricorn

You have scope to be even more outgoing and sociable than usual at the moment. The Sun presently occupies your solar ninth house, assisting you to put yourself at the head of things. At the same time you should relish the company of many different sorts of people – most of whom find you fascinating and good to have around.

3 WEDNESDAY
Moon Age Day 5   Moon Sign Aquarius

Your tongue and wit are both extremely sharp at present and whilst this can be a very positive trend, there is just a slight possibility that you could offer someone offence without realising you have done so. Maybe just a little more concern for the sensibilities of people in your vicinity is called for right now.

4 THURSDAY
Moon Age Day 6   Moon Sign Aquarius

The signs are that you may be more outgoing as the days slip by and can certainly put yourself in the limelight where social situations are concerned. For some reason your popularity is even higher now. It could be that you are presently encountering many different invitations and you will be loath to turn down any of them.

149

5 FRIDAY
Moon Age Day 7   Moon Sign Pisces

You can now get figures in positions of authority to notice you not by sucking up to them, but simply by making a positive impression. As a result you could be marked out for special treatment. Confidence remains especially high for Aries people who are career specialists.

6 SATURDAY
Moon Age Day 8   Moon Sign Pisces

With the Moon in your solar twelfth house at the moment it is possible that you become better at expressing sympathy and that your ability to see what makes others tick is more enhanced than usual. You can make today slightly quieter, particularly if you are happy to watch, wait and listen for a few hours.

7 SUNDAY
Moon Age Day 9   Moon Sign Pisces

The Moon remains in a position that highlights the more sensitive qualities within your nature. It also offers a quieter interlude and maybe a good time for planning. Don't forget that the busiest time of the year is just around the corner. And even if you don't like Christmas much yourself, those you care about probably do.

8 MONDAY
Moon Age Day 10   Moon Sign Aries

Your strength lies in inspired thinking, and with the lunar high present you can put many of your most important thoughts into action. It's time to get busy and to show everyone who you are and what you are capable of doing. On the way you can take advantage of more than your fair share of good luck.

9 TUESDAY
Moon Age Day 11   Moon Sign Aries

You can get most things to go your way, particularly if you are willing to take life by the scruff of the neck and shake it into what you want. There is a slightly ruthless streak about but as long as you look out for the good of others, as well as feathering your own nest, this shouldn't be much of a problem.

10 WEDNESDAY *Moon Age Day 12   Moon Sign Taurus*

Today offers you a boost to practical affairs and continues to work in your favour. If it seems you are somewhat short of cash you need to delve deep into your originality and to think up new ways to earn more. The upcoming Christmas season could now become a serious issue in your mind – somewhat belatedly, it might seem.

11 THURSDAY *Moon Age Day 13   Moon Sign Taurus*

Your need for better communication and your desire to get about more combine to indicate a restless but potentially interesting time. Trends encourage contact with loads of people, but the problem is that there are not enough hours in a day to achieve all your objectives. Patience, Aries – patience!

12 FRIDAY *Moon Age Day 14   Moon Sign Gemini*

There is much to gain from all co-operative ventures at this time and particularly so in the case of Aries people who are involved in business partnerships. Personal attachments are also well starred and it might be the magic of the season, but you can show yourself to be deeply romantic and more inclined to speak words of love.

13 SATURDAY *Moon Age Day 15   Moon Sign Gemini*

It might seem quite natural that social gatherings are on the increase, but present astrological trends would have encouraged this at any time of year. The Moon is now in your solar fourth house and that suggests more concern than usual about the welfare of family members. Good deeds are definitely your forte at the moment.

14 SUNDAY *Moon Age Day 16   Moon Sign Cancer*

You now have quicker access to information that can easily be turned to your advantage. If you are involved in some inward battle, for example stopping smoking or trying to control your weight, by all means keep up your efforts but at the same time avoid being quite as hard on yourself as might sometimes be the case.

15 MONDAY
Moon Age Day 17   Moon Sign Cancer

If you need more genuine fun and stimulating romance in your life at this time, the planets can help with this. Entertaining others is as simple as encountering them in social situations or else inviting them round to your home. People could find you absolutely fascinating to have around, and might be happy to tell you.

16 TUESDAY
Moon Age Day 18   Moon Sign Leo

You might be slightly more excitable today and could easily be over-reacting to situations that would normally not move you much at all. Avoid arguing simply for the sake of doing so, and whenever possible take the line of least resistance in discussions. If you shoot from the hip too much, you will probably regret the fact later.

17 WEDNESDAY
Moon Age Day 19   Moon Sign Leo

This could be an ideal time for travel and also for spiritual studies of almost any sort. There can be something quite introspective about you whilst the Sun remains in your solar ninth house, though this is a period that should only last for a few days more. It's worth talking to as many different sorts of people as proves to be possible today.

18 THURSDAY
Moon Age Day 20   Moon Sign Virgo

You may find it easy to bend career situations to your own advantage and can be quite persuasive, even with those who are in overall authority. Trends assist you to get things to go your way, both today and tomorrow. This is one of those periods when Aries is on a roll, but be careful because things could change by the weekend.

19 FRIDAY
Moon Age Day 21   Moon Sign Virgo

Your influence remains strong, and although Christmas is just around the corner, for today at least you can be fully committed to practical matters. The upcoming weekend might be much quieter and will offer time for reflection. However, for the moment your best approach is to plan well ahead and act on impulse.

20 SATURDAY
Moon Age Day 22   Moon Sign Libra

You may decide not to push yourself too hard today, or even leave your favourite chair if you have any choice in the matter. The lunar low encourages you to contemplate and to sit on the riverbank of life for a while, watching the water flow by. This is not a time for prohibitive actions.

21 SUNDAY
Moon Age Day 23   Moon Sign Libra

Practical setbacks are possible and if they come along all you can do is to deal with them one at a time. By tomorrow everything should look quite different, which is why it would be sensible to shelve certain jobs until later. If you don't, you could find yourself having to repeat them later in any case.

22 MONDAY
Moon Age Day 24   Moon Sign Scorpio

Today marks a time that is ideal when it comes to benefiting from any sort of research or in-depth study. Although the lunar low has now moved away, you may not be fully back on form, and would be wise to move cautiously towards some of your objectives. Oh, by the way, Christmas day is only three days away! Had you forgotten?

23 TUESDAY
Moon Age Day 25   Moon Sign Scorpio

Although Christmas is generally a time for families and close friendships, Aries has the ability to use the social gatherings in order to further professional objectives. This could certainly be the case today, particularly if you use your cheerful and happy nature to make a favourable impression on potentially influential people.

24 WEDNESDAY
Moon Age Day 26   Moon Sign Scorpio

Christmas Eve offers scope for expanding interests. There are planetary trends around that encourage you to give at least some time to the needs of family members, but you might still not be over-keen to give yourself to Christmas absolutely. By the evening you could be possessed by a warm glow and get more sentimental.

25 THURSDAY *Moon Age Day 27   Moon Sign Sagittarius*

Venus is in your solar eleventh house for Christmas Day and that assists you to be sociable, happy to mix with both family members and friends, and anxious to have a good time. What is more important is the way you treat other people. Nobody is kinder than the average Aries individual, and you can show the fact today.

26 FRIDAY *Moon Age Day 28   Moon Sign Sagittarius*

This is a day during which you can afford to vent some of your pent-up frustrations. These can probably be dispersed simply by getting a change of scenery and by enjoying something different from the Christmas norm. If the weather is good you might opt for a walk in the country or by the coast. Whatever you choose, variety is essential.

27 SATURDAY *Moon Age Day 0   Moon Sign Capricorn*

If there is something you need to say, now is the time to get it off your chest. You have a unique combination of skills at the moment. It will be possible for you to broach subjects that might have been taboo in the past, and at the same time you can show great kindness and a willingness to listen to another point of view.

28 SUNDAY *Moon Age Day 1   Moon Sign Capricorn*

If you happen to be working today you need to be aware of new opportunities for advancement. Most Aries people will still be in the midst of the festivities and if your time is your own, give some hours to thoughts about the future. Now is as good a time for planning as you are likely to encounter this month.

29 MONDAY *Moon Age Day 2   Moon Sign Capricorn*

The way to stay happy today is via social matters and group encounters. Aries needs company right now and relishes the cut and thrust of interesting and stimulating conversation. Even if not everyone seems to be on your side, you should be able to brush off any comments that seem custom-made to annoy you.

30 TUESDAY   *Moon Age Day 3   Moon Sign Aquarius*

You can attract attention through the speed with which you express
yourself at the moment, and can persuade others to be involved in
your present ideas. Your mind is already well into the New Year and
it is unlikely that you will be making too many resolutions. Aries
knows what it wants and plans well ahead to get it.

31 WEDNESDAY   *Moon Age Day 4   Moon Sign Aquarius*

The last day of the year could mean business as usual for many Aries
subjects. You can achieve positive dealings with a business partner and
show a great talent for commanding respect from almost anyone. You
remain, to the last moment of the year, a born organiser, sure of
yourself and happy to take on anything that looks lucrative.

RISING SIGNS FOR ARIES

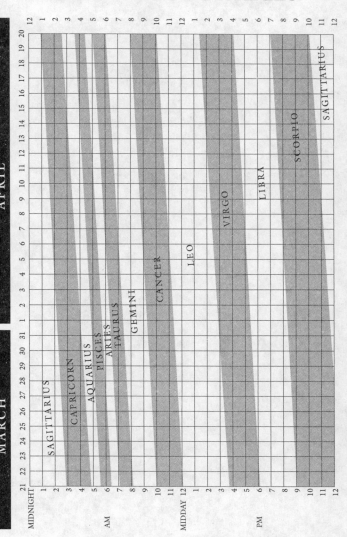

THE ZODIAC, PLANETS AND CORRESPONDENCES

The Earth revolves around the Sun once every calendar year, so when viewed from Earth the Sun appears in a different part of the sky as the year progresses. In astrology, these parts of the sky are divided into the signs of the zodiac and this means that the signs are organised in a circle. The circle begins with Aries and ends with Pisces.

Taking the zodiac sign as a starting point, astrologers then work with all the positions of planets, stars and many other factors to calculate horoscopes and birth charts and tell us what the stars have in store for us.

The table below shows the planets and Elements for each of the signs of the zodiac. Each sign belongs to one of the four Elements: Fire, Air, Earth or Water. Fire signs are creative and enthusiastic; Air signs are mentally active and thoughtful; Earth signs are constructive and practical; Water signs are emotional and have strong feelings.

It also shows the metals and gemstones associated with, or corresponding with, each sign. The correspondence is made when a metal or stone possesses properties that are held in common with a particular sign of the zodiac.

Finally, the table shows the opposite of each star sign – this is the opposite sign in the astrological circle.

Placed	Sign	Symbol	Element	Planet	Metal	Stone	Opposite
1	Aries	Ram	Fire	Mars	Iron	Bloodstone	Libra
2	Taurus	Bull	Earth	Venus	Copper	Sapphire	Scorpio
3	Gemini	Twins	Air	Mercury	Mercury	Tiger's Eye	Sagittarius
4	Cancer	Crab	Water	Moon	Silver	Pearl	Capricorn
5	Leo	Lion	Fire	Sun	Gold	Ruby	Aquarius
6	Virgo	Maiden	Earth	Mercury	Mercury	Sardonyx	Pisces
7	Libra	Scales	Air	Venus	Copper	Sapphire	Aries
8	Scorpio	Scorpion	Water	Pluto	Plutonium	Jasper	Taurus
9	Sagittarius	Archer	Fire	Jupiter	Tin	Topaz	Gemini
10	Capricorn	Goat	Earth	Saturn	Lead	Black Onyx	Cancer
11	Aquarius	Waterbearer	Air	Uranus	Uranium	Amethyst	Leo
12	Pisces	Fishes	Water	Neptune	Tin	Moonstone	Virgo